POSITIVE IN

5 Simple Actions to Eliminate the Negative and Embrace the Positive for an Amazing, Abundant & Revitalized Life

JOE MORTON

Published by
Sound Concepts
782 S. Auto Mall Dr. Ste A
American Fork, UT 84043 U.S.A.
801-225-9520

Copyright © 2016 by Joe Morton

All rights reserved. No part of this publication may be reproduced or distributed in any form or by any means, or stored in a data base or retrieval system, without the prior written permission of the author.

Designed by Sound Concepts
Printed in the United States of America

DEDICATION

I am grateful for my wife Caryn. Caryn is always first on my list of gratitude. You're my best friend and my closest confidant. I thoroughly enjoy experiencing life's incredible adventures with you. And, of course, our four children, Cayden, Ethan, Nathan and Kelsey, many thanks for inspiring and loving me.

I am also grateful for my mother and father, Gordon and Gabriella Morton. They truly have been mentors of mine and continue to always be there for me. To them, there was never anything that was not possible.

I want to express gratitude for my brothers and my sister: Gordon, David, Michael and Daniela for being such amazing siblings. Some of my greatest memories growing up and going forward to today involve you. Blessed.

I want to express gratitude to my business partners, Aaron, Gordon, Gary, Kent and Beverly. We have been through a lot and I would not want to be with any other partners. I love our business and I love our deep discussions on becoming all that we can become. With this group, there is always a way. Even after so many years in business you would think we would be sick of each other, but that's far from the truth. I can't wait to get together with my partners to discuss business, family, the books we are reading, life, or just a late night call to review the day and shoot the breeze (Aaron and I have had a few of those).

Life is amazing. Life is a blessing. Don't go a day without expressing gratitude to someone in your life who has helped you, even if it is the store clerk who did their job with a smile. We all make a difference.

Table of Contents

INTRODUCTION 7

CHAPTER 1 21

CHAPTER 2 31

CHAPTER 3 45

CHAPTER 4 63

CHAPTER 5 85

CHAPTER 6 99

CHAPTER 7 109

CONCLUSION 153

INTRODUCTION

The Hero's Journey

I love American scholar Joseph Campbell's brilliant description of the hero's journey, which is a pattern of narrative that appears in drama, storytelling, myth, religious ritual, and psychological development. On the journey the hero goes out, is tested through severe challenges and ordeals, finds great reward and ultimately experiences great personal growth as he or she achieves great deeds on behalf of the group, tribe, or civilization.

We all have our own journeys in life that we must take. It is up to us whether we want to embrace the journey and in the process become who we are supposed to be.

My Journey

My parents taught me that anything is possible in life. My mother was an Italian immigrant who moved with her family to Ontario

Canada after WWII. She was very loving but firm and did not allow us to feel too sorry for ourselves. She had always seen much more challenging things than we were experiencing. It's hard to argue with an immigrant mother who lived her early years in war-torn Europe. My father was a very hard working, school-of-hard-knocks sort of father, very self-taught. He was always reading one or two or even three books at a time. (Still does to this day.) He had an amazing appetite for learning and bettering his mind and life. He learned and continues to learn from the best of the best.

My parents were early pioneers in the health and wellness movement. They were into herbal supplements, purified drinking water, carob instead of chocolate, chiropractors, no-sugar diets, no white flour, enemas, reading eyes, and hormone-free meat long before such things were hip. Before there was a store called Sprouts, my parents grew sprouts in our kitchen. (It was always very interesting to go to school in the 1970s and have sprouts in your sandwich. We were the kids I am sure no one wanted to trade lunches with.)

My parents were constantly educating themselves—and us—on the human body and what could be done to maximize our health from a holistic manner. This included having a healthy mind. If you were to walk into our home you would find Herbally Yours, the book by Penny Royal, and close to it, As a Man Thinketh by James Allen, or How to Win Friends and Influence People by Dale Carnegie. I did not always appreciate the education that I was getting while growing up. Not going trick-or-treating for Halloween is disturbing for a child, and learning the effects of an herb called cascara sagrada firsthand can be embarrassing. However, one of the of the most important things I learned from my parents was that our bodies are capable of healing in ways that we cannot truly appreciate.

I also learned that our minds are remarkably powerful. What we plant in our minds will sprout for good or bad. My parents took us to seminars like those given by Bob Proctor. I had the chance to learn that we are capable of accomplishing anything we put our minds to. I did not realize at the time that the beliefs I was absorbing at such an early age would truly shape my life. I did not always appreciate it then, but how blessed I feel now.

As an adult, I became busy with school and building a career. I had to learn the hard way that what we put in our mouths in the form of food really does matter. I woke up in my late 20s wondering how I was so out of shape. I couldn't run more than a mile. I was shocked. I wasn't overweight, nor did I have any serious health conditions that I knew of, but I could sense the early warning signs. I tried to imagine my life 5, 10, 20 years in the future and realized that if I didn't make changes I was heading down a path to misery. So, I started to make changes and saw incredible advances in my health. It ultimately guided me toward being a founding partner in a health and wellness company. I addressed my physical body but neglected my mind.

The company I helped start experienced incredible success. But with success, challenges crept in. Sometimes they didn't just creep in, they poured in. I never stopped working. My phone was with me every moment of every day. Vacations were work trips. Date nights were filled with work. I loved my business but I was burning the candle at both ends and from the middle. My travel schedule was intense. It seemed like I was in a perpetual state of jet lag. Anxiety would begin to build hours and even days before I needed to travel.

The toughest part was that my partners and I had to battle a series of corporate lawsuits that took their toll on me. They became very personal to me, they were made public, and they went on for years. I saw a side of business that I did not like and had a difficult time accepting. I saw friends of many years turn on each other, all in the name of business. Was it worth it? I could not make sense of it.

On top of all that, our business faced a series of other challenges. A few top salespeople had sudden accidents resulting in death, our IT systems temporarily collapsed and put a halt to our business, we had manufacturing difficulties, international market disturbances, competitor attacks, and then the financial crisis started in 2007. Additionally, I found myself being so negative. It was as if a foggy cloud of pessimism was always around me. I was able to hide it from most, but it was definitely there. I tried getting rid of it, but it was like pushing a boulder up a hill. I felt like I was in a perpetual "spiral" of negativity. I did not like this side of myself. I wanted so much to find happiness and my bliss again. But how?

In all, I felt like I was playing a real-life version of "whack-a-mole." I could never quite get caught up with any one issue, and I was suffering.

A few close people understood what I was going through, most notably my wife and my partners at work. We all found ourselves hungering to find peace despite the pain that the lawsuits and other challenges were causing. I was becoming jaded and I did not like that. I found that it was increasingly more difficult to handle even the smallest of life's ups and downs. Sleep became a luxury that was simply no longer there. I also started to develop stomach challenges as a result of the constant stress and inability to sleep. My patience wasn't what it had been in the past. My marriage was strong, my family was amazing, I had wonderful and supportive partners in my business, but more and more I found myself feeling anxious about the future. I felt lonely. I dreaded getting on a plane to travel anywhere—airplanes were like isolation chambers. Hotel rooms felt like a prison. Some of the only times I would feel peace were when my wife would hug me and hold me. But sadly, I found myself rejecting my wife's loving touch. I was so frustrated with life that I did not know what to do. I started feeling hopeless and I didn't understand what was happening to me. I had always been a person who marveled at the simple things in life. So what had changed? I wanted so much to regain my love of life. I wanted so badly to once again stop and smell the roses and feel peace and comfort. How could I be doing the right thing physically—eating well, getting plenty of exercise and so forth—but be so emotionally drained? It was clear that my physical health woes were a result of my stress, but I had no answers. I was feeding my body the right things physically, but emotionally I was becoming bankrupt.

It was during this time of tremendous struggle that I realized I had stopped feeding my mind what it needed to handle life's challenges. I had been living off what my parents had taught me years earlier. Sure, I had read some of the books, or at least knew what they taught because my father would perpetually quote them to us while we growing up. What I had forgotten, however, is that, just like in the saying, "an apple a day keeps the doctor away," it is not an apple a week, or a month, or a year, or in this case, years. I was feeding my body the right nutrition, but I was not feeding my mind. Just like with my physical health, I needed to go back to the basics of feeding my emotional, spiritual and mental health each and every day. My spirit craved nutrition. My spirit craved positive material so that positivity could affect all the roles that I needed to play. I realized that my wife and kids needed me strong. My business partners and company needed me at my best. I was needed. But how to start?

Several years earlier, I had set a goal to climb Kilamanjaro, the highest peak on the African continent. I went with my buddy Lance and my son Cayden. It was an amazing experience that helped me discover what was lacking in my life.

While in our tent one evening, my son pulled out a copy of "As A Man Thinketh" by James Allen. He had just finished reading it. I was intrigued that he had this book, so I asked if I could read it. I devoured that book. My mind and soul were so thirsty that the book filled them quickly. One of the most compelling truths I found in the book was this: "Of all the beautiful truths pertaining to the soul which have been restored and brought to light in this age, none is more gladdening or fruitful of divine promise and confidence than this—that man is the master of thought, the moulder of character and the maker and shaper of condition, environment and destiny."

I realized that it was up to me. I controlled me. I needed to want it and I did. It was a start. Much like a muscle that's rarely used, my mind was atrophying. I knew I needed to strengthen my mind. And I also discovered that partaking in the mental and emotional feeding should not be, as I said, "An apple a month," but rather something we participate in on a daily basis.

As I came to this realization, I understood that we are all needed. You, my friend, are important. You are surrounded by people who need you. I believe there truly is a force that connects each and every one of us and, if we can understand how to tap into this force, transformation begins, starting with us and then flowing to others who are open to change. This force can be felt by others and change can occur in them if they are ready and desiring to receive. If any of my journey sounds familiar to you, I invite you to join me and learn how you can free your mind and move towards healing. I experience life slowing down as I soak in all that life has to offer. I love life and I want to invite you to do the same.

Turn Within

There are hundreds of books that offer amazing wisdom and advice. I love them and read them regularly, and I encourage others to do the same. However, many of these books promote programs, "to-do" lists or fairly complex behaviors that require significant time and commitment. I'm not saying these programs or lists of behaviors aren't good or worthwhile. I simply feel that in the face of so many recommendations, it might be easy for the average person to become confused or paralyzed with indecision. Rather, I would have you instead focus first on learning to "turn within" and recognize that you are capable of overcoming and bringing about significant improvement in your life. Then, incorporating some of the recommended programs, lists and behaviors of others won't be such a daunting task. And remember, these things can certainly help you, but at the end of the day it is you who will bring about the change. And you, my friend, are powerful beyond comprehension.

I could chose from countless quotes, verses or talks given on this subject to make this point, but I want to draw your attention to a recently discovered and studied text of ancient origin attributed to a great teacher, Jesus Christ. In 1896, a German scholar named Karl Reinhardt purchased a papyrus scroll in Cairo, Egypt. After this finding, two other fragments were discovered. Many scholars believe the original text is dated to around the 2nd century but some believe it was written during the time of Jesus's ministry. This codex Pa- pyrus Berolinensis 8502 is called the Gospel of Mary (as in Mary Magdalene). It is a very interesting read and one that is debated in Christianity. However, debating its origin and authenticity is not my purpose with quoting it. I simply love what is said in the following verse that was attributed to Jesus speaking to Mary:

"Peace be with you! Acquire my peace. Be careful not to let anyone mislead you by saying, 'Look over here!' or 'Look over there!' Because the Authentic Person exists within you. Follow that person! Those who seek will find."

I find this to be very beautiful. What an amazing statement. It is within all of us. It is within you. This tells me that as we become present, as we learn how to turn within as so many great teachers have shared over the thousands of years of recorded history, we will find answers. Those who "seek will find." I believe the principles of Take 5 will help us seek and will help us find. A big part of this is learning how and practicing becoming present in our lives. I recommend it daily. As we recognize that we are the ones to truly create change, we will be more open to learn from these great authors, programs and systems of change and learning that are in abundance around us.

"The world within is governed by mind. When we discover this world we shall find the solution for every problem, the cause for every effect; and since the world within is subject to our control, all laws of power and possession are also within our control."

– Charles Haanal

You Can Choose to Be Happy

One other thing. For many years, I had a belief that success in life (and the happiness that would supposedly accompany that success) generally meant money, material goods and business "success." That particular house, car, watch or whatever material item meant success and happiness. What I have learned is this—money and material goods are great but are simply are a byproduct of success. Success, as Earl Nightingale states, is the progressive realization of a worthy ideal. I like this idea because it is not tied to material goods but rather to moving forward In the direction of a worthy goal or dream and making the world a better place.

I thought "success" in the form of money and business would take away my problems. I believe this is a thought that most of us have. The world —television, movies, magazines, books, the general media—tells us to believe that life with money frees us and makes us happy. This is not true. What I have learned over the years is that money doesn't necessarily make us happy. Money will simply amplify what and who we are within.

Let's take happiness as an example. Happiness is a choice and can be found whether we have money or not. This is why you will find happy people who have money, and also will find miserable people who have money. This is why you will find happy people who don't have a lot of money, and unhappy people who don't have a lot of money. I have learned that money doesn't take away challenges, but rather it can promote the creation of new and different ones. This is why we need to learn how to address what is happening within, to have that inner peace bring forth the outer peace that we all desire. Life is not meant to be an experience free of challenges. Challenges will always be there in one form or another. It is how we respond to those challenges that determines if we live free or not. It is freedom of our mind that creates true freedom, and as we free our minds we experience freedom, no matter what we are experiencing in life, good or bad. As we free our minds then peace is uncovered, no matter what our financial situation may be.

Freedom of the mind is creating harmony and peace. Freedom of the mind means quieting the EGO. The EGO will try to tell you that money and material goods are not a byproduct of success but are rather success itself, and you that need these things to make yourself accepted in society. Your EGO will tell you that you need it to look better than others. Your EGO will say you need "it" —whatever "it" is—because if you don't have "it" then you can't "keep up with the Joneses."

As you quiet the EGO, these feelings begin to disappear. You'll begin to express more gratitude for that which you have and find true happiness wherever you may be in life, whatever you may be driving, in whatever house you may be in because you are progressing with your worthy ideal. Quiet the EGO and you will find driving that car, living in that house, wearing those clothes is now an experience of gratitude and love rather than an experience of "what are others thinking of me?" Positive IN and the Take 5 steps comprise a process of quieting the EGO so true harmony and peace can be found in all the roles that we play in life."

Who Is This Book For?

Who is this book for? It is for everyone. Every person can benefit from this book. Allow me to highlight a few people who could learn from this book. Of course, these are not the only people, but are just examples of the types of people who could benefit from the book.

Relationship – Are you in a relationship? How much more effective could your communications be if you spoke positive and kind words to one another and knew that your significant other could trust you to speak kind words and positive things about you outside of your presence? How much better would your day be, knowing you spoke words of love to your spouse or significant other? How would your day go and how would his or her day go? How would your romance be if you went into a date with a positive outlook on the evening? What if you spoke words of encouragement, love, and gratitude? I will be discussing these things and more. This book is for you.

Father or Mother – When I think of the most important roles in society, parenthood is right at the top of the list. The family is where so much of the early teaching takes place and it greatly influences how our children view life. How much more effective could you be as a parent if each day you sent your children off to school and/or work with the attitude that anything is possible? What if you instilled in them an attitude that there is always a solution to whatever life throws their way? How much more resilient would your kids be if each day was spent filling your mind and theirs with positivity? It breaks my heart when I hear a mother say something like, "I am just a stay at home mother," or "I make no difference in this world as a father or mother." You do make a difference and the world needs you strong to raise our world's next generation of leaders. This book is for you.

Health and Wellness – Do you have certain fitness goals? Certain weight management goals? Do you want to be in better shape? Do you want to fit into that dress or suit again? Do you want to accomplish a 5K, 10K, half or full marathon? How about a triathlon? Do you want to climb a mountain? How about having more energy each day to accomplish all that you have to accomplish? How about just improving your health for the heck of having better health? You can do it. It is reachable. This book is for you.

Student – If we become what we think about, would it not make sense to start your days off correctly with an attitude of success and seeing yourself as a successful student? Seeing yourself understanding the material, accomplishing the homework assignments and becoming who you are meant to become during the process of school? Imagine comprehending and truly learning the material. This book is for you.

New Job – You are just starting a job. You are the new kid on the block, so to speak. You want to do a good job. You want to come in with fresh ideas and grow with the company. You want to make a good impression. You want to feel like you are making a difference. This book is for you.

Middle Management – You want to lead your team to success. You want to make a difference in the sales of your organization. You want to take your career to the next level and become a vice president or C-level employee. You want to be sure to hit your budgets and succeed with whatever project is placed in your department. You want to make a difference. This book is for you.

Upper management – You are charged with the responsibility of growing your company. You have the responsibility of profit and loss and the balance sheet. Entire departments depend on you to be on your "A" game at any given point. People depend on your ideas and expertise so the company can succeed, month in and month out. People look up to you. People make decisions from watching you, whether you realize it or not. Your very actions help people make life decisions. This book is for you.

Entrepreneur – The world needs you. The world depends on you as an entrepreneur. The whole purpose of going through the schooling system is, of course, to learn, but also to get a job. And who creates the jobs? There is no magical job-creating machine that churns out employment opportunities for all the students graduating each and every year. It is you, the entrepreneur, who are creating the jobs. Do you realize how valuable you are to our economy? Every company was a startup at one point or another. Every brand started with a dreamer. As James Allen stated, "The dreamers are the saviors of the world. As the visible world is sustained by the invisible, so men, through all their trials and sins and sordid vocations, are nourished by the beautiful visions of their solitary dreamers. Humanity cannot forget its dreamers." You are the dreamers. We depend on you to find a need and think how you can offer a solution to this need. This can be in the form of a "first to market" or simply finding a way to do something better. Either way, we need you to be strong. We need you to see the world in a positive light and bring your dreams to the market place. Dreamers think out of the box. This is where most ideas come from – out of the box. It requires a person to think differently and thinking differently in society can be a challenge. Starting a company is not always easy. It takes a lot of effort. Keep your dreams alive. This book is for you.

Media – There is a huge need for people involved in media to be positive. Please forgive me for speaking about the negative influence the media can have on society. This is more as a whole and not individually. With media, I feel that your approach can make a difference in how we receive the messages. We all know and admire certain broadcasters who seem to have a positive glow about them. We need you. This book is for you.

Salespeople – My brother Gordon once said, "A sale takes place when need meets opportunity." A good salesperson understands this. A good salesperson helps a person with a need and connects them with an opportunity. Our buying habits are influenced by a good salesperson who can help us make a purchase to meet our needs. I recently wanted to trade in my vehicle and get a new one. I went into the dealership and explained what I was looking for. The salesperson was very difficult to speak to. He was tough to track down. When it came to negotiations, he was not willing to discuss the terms. I told him I knew I could get the terms I was looking for because I had done my research. He was quite cold about it and would not even discuss it with me. I said I appreciated his time and told him I was going to another dealership to purchase a vehicle. He wished me well. Within a few days I was driving the exact vehicle I wanted with even better terms than I was expecting and options that I hadn't known I would enjoy so much. All because of a good salesperson who cared about what I was looking for and would not rest until I had the car I wanted and better terms than I asked for. I went to three different dealerships and one did the best job of connecting me with what I wanted. As Covey would say, "Win-win." We need good, positive salespeople. This book is for you.

Educators – The world needs you. Next to learning in the home, schools are where our children learn. They learn reading and writing, mathematics, health, science, English, other languages, music, fitness etc. This is the basis of a life of learning and growing. We can all think back on the teachers who did not just "teach" us, but truly "reached" us, the ones who gave us comfort and helped us see the world in a positive light. We remember the teachers who recognized our talents and took the time to try a new approach that made the difference in our learning. We appreciate the teachers who cared for us enough to help us truly learn. What an important role teachers play in our society. Educators have great power and influence. We need you to be positive each and every day. That is a lot to ask. God bless you all. I thank you for making a difference. You are the one who takes our children on a journey of learning and growth. Again, we need you positive and looking for new ideas and solutions to educate. This book is for you.

Network Marketers – This could be placed in the category of sales; however, networkers build teams that span towns, cities, states, country borders and the globe. It is easy to quit in any type of sales function, yet we rely on the salesperson so we need you strong. We need this form of distribution that allows any person from any walk of life the chance to succeed. Networking and sales are not concerned about what your GPA was, what you studied or did not study in school, whether you are from one side of town or the other, the color of your skin, male or female, or young or old. The opportunity is for everyone who has a dream alive and wanting to be dusted off and pursued. Anyone can join and success is available to all. This book is for you.

Store Clerk – Do you recognize how much of an influence you can have in your position? You don't know what is going on in a person's life before they showed up at your store. You don't know what conversation they just had with a friend or loved one. You are not aware of what is happening with their health or at work. Because of that, the simple act of a smile, or asking about their day or their children, or giving them a compliment could have a huge impact. Remember that happiness is contagious. Positivity is contagious. This book is for you.

Restaurant Server – I'm just a server, what difference can I make? You may be tempted to repeat these words or thoughts. Be careful, you make a huge difference for good or for bad. I served tables at multiple restaurants in Canada where I grew up and I loved the experience. People come in to dine for all different reasons. It may simply be to fuel their body, which is a need and you help fulfill that need. However, for dinner particularly, many come in to let their hair down, so to speak. They are there with a significant other or with a group. They may be out on a date or celebrating a special time in their life. Whatever it may be, a restaurant can and should act as an escape from the world and their lives for a moment in time. It can and should be a sanctuary where people can come and check their challenges at the door for a brief time and enter the world of culinary bliss and enjoy the special discussions and time with others. A good server understands this and helps their clients experience a break from life and uplifts them. We need you positive. This book is for you.

To start seeing life and all it has to offer in a positive light doesn't happen overnight. Life itself often seems to be pulling us in a negative direction. To counteract this, I invite you to read a chapter of this book each day. You can read more of course, but the purpose is to create a habit or ritual of feeding your mind and soul on a daily basis with Positive IN material. This book is about changing daily habits and getting on a road to seeing the abundance this world has to offer and how important you are in the world.

CHAPTER 1

PIPO: Positive In, Positive Out

GIGO is a computer science acronym for "Garbage in, Garbage out." The dictionary.com definition of GIGO is: "A rule stating that when faulty data are fed into a computer, the information that emerges will also be faulty." In other words, computers do what they are programmed to do; if the output is wrong, it's because the computer was programmed that way. We, as human beings, are very similar to a computer. If we program our minds with negativity, (garbage) then negativity (garbage) will come out. GIGO. But the opposite is also true! If we program our minds and hearts with positivity (Positive In), then positive will come out (Positive Out). I guess we can call it PIPO.

I play many roles in my life: husband, father, neighbor, friend, service roles in my community, investor, entrepreneur, and business owner. I also have many pastimes and passions such as guitar, running, triathlons, skiing, rock and ice climbing, mountaineering and travel. I need to be "on" to help me fulfill the roles and passions

Start Your Day Right

Start your day off right by turning off the negative and inviting the positive through Taking 5. You are in control. It is as if you are sitting in front of the TV with hundreds of channels to watch and you have control with the click of a button. You can choose something positive or you can get sucked into the negative, such as the news or some violent show.

Here is the interesting thing. Have you ever noticed that the longer you dwell on something negative the harder it seems to break away? You know instinctively that it is hurting your inner guidance system but the longer you watch the more difficult it is to break away. It makes us dull.

So you have a choice. It is within you to turn the dial so to speak. Just recognize that the longer you dwell on the negative, the stronger your negative vibrational energy will be and the harder it will be to switch the channel. The opposite is also true. The longer you dwell on the positive, the stronger your positive vibrational energy will be. Make the decision first thing every morning to tune your channels into positive and stay tuned all day. You may find yourself going out of tune to the negative stations. When you find this happening, simply Take 5. As you get more experienced with this practice you will be able to tune yourself back into the positive quite quickly.

in my life, so I have had a chance to put PIPO to the test over and over and over again. I am here to tell you, it works—both ways. Hard though it is to admit, I have spent time in my life putting garbage into my mind and the outcome was garbage (GIGO). I have also worked hard to put positive in and the outcome was positive (PIPO)! Our minds truly are like computers, but unfortunately, we tend to overlook what our minds are capable of accomplishing. The human mind is an absolute miracle. We really do go in the direction of whatever is dominating our thoughts.

The thing we need to realize is that all too often we are programming our minds to think we are less than what we are capable of becoming. You may say, "No, I can't do that. I'm not capable." Well, consider this: If you wake up and one of the first things you do is to watch the news or read the news or both, what did you program into your mind to start your day? Mostly negative, because the news is mostly negative. I have tested this on my own and continue to experience the same results. Scan through the morning news and do your own test. I have also at times included sports channels. They are often filled with men and women yelling at each other. Again, negative.

If a good majority of people start their days by reading or watching the news, then they take that negative viewpoint out into the world, to the office or to school or wherever they are going. What will be the outcome? Conversations are often created throughout the day based around whatever the news and media are promoting. "Did you hear that statistic about murders in our country/state/city?" "I knew our president was a crook." "Speaking of crooks, all bankers are crooks. So are the lawyers who represent the bankers." "Oh my goodness, did you hear about that person in the NBA, or NFL, or actor?" "Did you see that report on cancer and how it is on the rise? I hope I don't get cancer. Is that a lump on my skin?" I recognize not all media is negative, but negativity tends to dominate and it gives us something juicy to talk about. Such topics take us to the end of our day when we watch the nightly news at around 10pm. What are we

The Butterfly Effect

You have the ability to change the course of not only your day and your life, but the lives of those around you. The difference that daily habits and rituals can make in your life and the lives of those you associate with is like the Butterfly Effect. The Butterfly Effect is defined by Dr. David Hawkins as "the law of sensitive dependence on initial conditions. This refers to the fact that an extremely minute variation over a course of time can have the effect of a profound change, much as a ship whose bearing is one degree off compass will eventually find itself hundreds of miles off course." It is crucial to understand that your actions have an impact.

then filling our minds with before we lay our heads down to sleep? More negativity. So we start our days with putting "garbage in," we oftentimes feed ourselves with garbage and gossip during the day, and then we end our day with putting "garbage in."

If it is true that "like attracts like" and "birds of a feather flock together," and if we are filling our minds with negative material, then we are walking around like a magnet that attracts the negativity in the world. No wonder we so often feel like we are on a treadmill and that we never seem to get ahead. No wonder we feel so run down. No wonder so many people feel hopeless and like there is no chance for them to ever accomplish anything great. No wonder so many dreams are left collecting dust on a shelf at home. The negativity we feed our minds sucks the desire out of us.

Life can be challenging, no doubt about it. I have yet to find one person who has found success in any area of their life who says that life is a breeze and there are never problems. Challenges will happen. Change will happen. But it is how we approach and view the challenges that help define us. It doesn't have to be hopeless. In fact, I am crazy enough to believe that we have the ability, like an inner guidance system, or as Gregg Braden says, a technology, within ourselves to transform our average day into something positive and amazing. We can, through certain daily habits or rituals, make sure that each day starts, continues and ends positively. That is what this book is about. Here is the truth—you are important. Your dreams are important. The world needs you. This book is about starting your journey to a more positive life, even if the beginning is seemingly very small. Start now and watch an amazing transformation over time.

TAKE 5

I want to introduce to you a quick fix that you can start right here and right now. I call it "Take 5" and it is a starting point toward positivity. "Take 5" stands for five things that you can do in five minutes. I recommend you practice "taking 5" first thing in the morning and, if needs be, throughout the day and then right before bed. There are entire chapters dedicated to these subjects, and we'll discuss them throughout the book. Repetition is good.

You will find "Take 5" so amazing that it may be tough to keep it to five minutes, but in the beginning at least, keep it to five and become comfortable with the ritual. It can be expanded over time until the day you discover that it is happening automatically. "Take 5" is as follows:

1. Gratitude. List as many things as you can in one minute that you are grateful for. This helps set up your mind and internal guidance system to be open and calm. The world of marketing tends to teach that happiness is found in the next "thing;" we can quickly get caught up in focusing on what we don't have. This minute is meant to remind you of what you do have—don't hold back. Include family members, loved ones, neighbors, friends, your health, your job, a person you work with who makes you laugh, your pet or favorite animal, your house, your food, clothing, schooling, your bike. There is no wrong answer. Heck, put down your garage door opener if it is something you are passionate about. This is your gratitude list. Enjoy the liberating feeling that gratitude can bring into your life. This can be done in the form of a prayer or just list it on a paper or in meditation. Your choice. It is your time and your list.

2. Love. This can and should go together with gratitude. Use the word love when thinking of the things you love about your life. For example, I love my wife and my four children. I invite you to include yourself. This can be difficult for many people. The golden rule states, "Love thy neighbor as thyself." How can we love our neighbor or truly love anything in our lives if we do not love ourselves? Consider that. This can also be done in the form of prayer or mediation or just making a list. Your choice. It is your list of loves.

3. Be in the Moment ("Be Still"). Meditating can easily be part of your process for steps 1 and 2 (love and gratitude). However, it can be separate as well. Our lives are so remarkably busy. Peace and healing are found when we quiet our minds. Try it. It can be tough to do with as busy a world as ours is. Try one minute of focusing on something you want to become in your thinking. I propose the word "abundance." Try to focus on this word for one minute. Abundance of love, abundance of happiness, abundance of patience, abundance of success, abundance of ideas, etc. Abundance is far reaching; there is abundance all around.

4. Read. Spend one minute reading something positive and uplifting, something that will help you be more optimistic. How would the world be if every person filled his or her mind with optimism at the beginning of each day? It would be a very different place. You may be wondering, where do I start? There are so many great authors and books out there. I have many listed in this book in other chapters, but I recommend one for all to have in their library. It is easy to read and one that can be read over and over. I have a copy of this book on my desk and I read from it almost daily. James Allen wrote As a Man Thinketh in 1903 and it is as powerful today as it

Happy = Healthy

It is clinically proven that optimistic people are healthier and happier than pessimists. In fact, the findings by researcher Sonja Lyubomirsky show that, among other things, happy people live 7-10 years longer than unhappy people, and optimistic people have a 77% lower risk of heart disease than pessimistic people.

(The How of Happiness, Sonja Lyubomirsky, 2012)

Turn Off the Negative

As you learn to "Take 5," I invite you to shut off the news (or at least limit its exposure). I know this can be a little tough for some but it will help limit your daily fear and negativity feeding. I also recommend you be very cautious with what you allow into your mind by way of entertainment. This can cause fear, worry and anxiety. In short, reject negativity.

was when it was written. (There is also a version titled As a Woman Thinketh. It is the same book but with words that reflect a female perspective, which I think was very wise to do.) This book will help set you up with the right emotions and thought processes to take on your day. I will also list many of my favorite books in the chapter on reading. Stay tuned.

5. Dream. Going through the first four steps of "Take 5" will help you prepare for the fifth step, which is to dream. As you emphasize gratitude, love, being present in the moment and reading as parts of your daily habits and rituals, it will help prepare you and your faith and belief will grow. As a result you will not only be allowed to dream, but also to keep your dreams and goals constantly at the forefront of everything you do. Dreams, goals and thoughts associated with emotion will help keep you in the direction of fulfillment and lasting change. This is why gratitude, love, being present and filling your mind with positive emotions and material is crucial for change and the dream-building and dream-fulfilling process.

Write down the dreams you have for your life that have not come true. And don't fall into the trap of believing that dreams don't come true. I am here to tell you that is bad programming. It is a limiting belief that needs to be reprogrammed for you. Dreams do come true. The world depends on dreams to bring forth ideas, products, brands, and companies. With all those things come jobs and opportunities. No one is here to put you down. No one is telling you to get your head out of the clouds. This is your time. We are meant to dream, and when we stop dreaming it is the beginning of the end.

One of the objectives of this book is to help shift our daily habits to correct our emotions and thoughts when needed. If your positive attitude starts to slip, as it sometimes does with each of us, remember to "Take 5" again in the afternoon. As you do this, magic will begin to happen. Challenges will not be so daunting. Rather than having a meltdown and finding yourself in the fetal position, you will be able to think of ways to overcome the obstacles. Before going to bed, stay away from the news. Be careful not to fill your mind with negative emotions and fears before sleep. This includes violent and negative programming that can enter our lives in the form of entertainment. Our minds cannot tell the difference between what is "fake" and what is real. Dr. David Hawkins said, "The major limitation of consciousness is its innocence. Consciousness is gullible, it believes what it hears. Consciousness is like hardware that will play back any software that is put into it. Its only guardian is a discerning awareness that scrutinizes the incoming program." We need to feed our minds and souls with positive emotions and feelings before shutting down, getting into a deep sleep that will allow our body to repair the way it is intended to. ==Don't feed the fears and negative emotions, but rather starve them with positive emotions. Power your positivity, belief and dreams instead.==

As we feed our conscious mind with daily positive material, we begin the process of changing the limiting beliefs that have been programmed into our subconscious mind. Doing so helps change the direction we are going in our lives. We become that which dominates our thoughts because we are changing the programming of what we believe is possible in life.

If you adhere to the principles in this book, you will find that your life is meant to be abundant—abundance of happiness, kindness, generosity, energy, love, joy, peace, dreams, ideas, solutions, relationships, health and wellness, education, personal development, laughter, smiles, overcoming of adversity, money and opportunities. Welcome to a journey in finding daily happiness and a positive outlook no matter what life has in store for you. Welcome to the world of Positive In, so positive can flow out in all the roles that you play.

CHAPTER 2

We Become What We Think About

People can be successful in so many different areas—politics, religion, business, science, writing, acting and sports are just a few. Earl Nightingale explains that regardless of where success comes from, and despite what differences they may have in the way they see the world, there seems to be something all successful people can agree on: we become what we think about.

Here are a few examples that illustrate this principle:

"The world within is the cause, the world without the effect; to change the effect you must change the cause." Charles Haanel

"There is a law in psychology that if you form a picture in your mind of what you would like to be, and you keep and hold that picture there long enough, you will soon become exactly as you have been thinking". William James

"For as [a man] thinketh in his heart, so is he." Proverbs 23:7

"A man is but the product of his thoughts. What he thinks, he becomes." Gandhi

"Attitudes are not the result of success. Success is result of attitudes." Earl Nightingale

"If your mental attitude is positive, even when threats abound, you won't lose your inner peace. On the other hand, if your mind is negative, marked by fear, suspicion and feelings of helplessness, even among your best friends, in a pleasant atmosphere and comfortable surroundings you won't be happy." Dalai Lama

"Happiness is an attitude. We either make ourselves miserable or happy and strong. The amount of work is the same." Francesca Reigler

"A man is what he thinks about all day long." Ralph Waldo Emerson

"The greatest discovery of my generation is that human beings can alter their lives by altering their attitudes of mind." William James

"People are always blaming their circumstances for what they are. I don't believe in circumstances. The people who get on in this world are the people who get up and look for the circumstances they want, and if they can't find them, make them." George Bernard Shaw

"What we are today comes from our thoughts of yesterday and our present thoughts build our life of tomorrow. Our life is the creation of our mind." Buddha

"Men believe that thought can be kept secret but it cannot. It rapidly crystallizes into habit and habit solidifies into circumstances." James Allen

"When a seed is planted in the ground, all you can do is water it. You cannot control the sunshine, you cannot control the weather, you cannot control whether the locust will come and try to destroy it. All you can do is plant your seed in the ground and water it and believe. That is what allowed me to be in this position right now. I would not stop believing." Tyler Perry

"The mind is everything. What you think you become." Buddha

"I know for sure that what we dwell on is who we become." Oprah Winfrey

"With every experience, you alone are painting your own canvas; thought by thought, choice by choice." Oprah Winfrey

"What we imagine in our minds becomes our world."
Dr. Masaru Emoto

"The observer effect in quantum physics states that where you place your attention is where you place your energy. As a consequence you affect the material world. If you entertain that idea even for a moment, you might start focusing on what you want instead of what you don't want." Dr. Joe Dispenza

"In my mind I have always been an A-list, Hollywood superstar. Y'all just didn't know yet." Will Smith

I could go on and on, but the point is made. We become what we think about. So what do you think about? How do you view yourself? How do you view your life? How do you view your family? How to you view your home? How do you view your job and career? How do you view the possibilities within your job and career? How do you view your dreams? Do you still seek to dream? Do you feel that life is abundance? How do you feel about your children's possibilities and dreams? Do you have hope for a better future? Do you recognize your worth?

We are greatly influenced by what is happening in our dominant thoughts. William Atkinson, in his book Thought Vibrations, calls this the law of attraction. He says, "Not only do our thoughts influence ourselves and others, but they have a drawing power—they attract to us the thoughts of others… in accord with the character of the thought uppermost in our minds. Thoughts of love will attract to us the love of others—circumstances and surroundings in accord with the thought; people who are of like thought."

In other words, if I have positive thoughts, those thoughts will attract positive thoughts from other people. We attract likeness. Watch society now that we are discussing this. I invite you to observe with whom people associate; it is uncanny. People who espouse a positive outlook attract other positive people who approach life the same way. Negative people tend to cluster together. Runners tend to find each other. Outdoor enthusiasts gravitate towards one another. Gamers find each other. Like-minded people gather; like-minded people feed off each other, for good or for bad. And they can infect each other, for good or for bad.

I want to give you an example from my life. I practice the law of attraction in my life each and every day, and without any doubt it works and is very real. I play a lot of sports and always have. I grew up playing hockey, baseball, basketball, some volleyball, skiing, and track and field. As an adult I have taken up such sports as triathlon, marathon, ultra marathon, rock climbing, ice climbing, mountaineering and hiking. I practice the law of attraction in all these areas. But one sport I have avoided like the plague is golf. I have played golf over the years but only in tournaments where it was best ball. Anyone can get a few good shots during 18 holes. I also appreciated the tournaments where they give you the licorice sticks to help you out on your putting. But for the most part, I would have rather had my eyeballs tattooed than play golf. The crazy thing was that I was a member of a golf club, and I had never even played there. I pretty much avoided the club and always had an excuse for why I never went.

If there was ever a way for me to put the law of attraction to the test, golf would be it. If it is true that we really go in the direction of what dominates our thoughts, then I decided I would let golf dominate my thoughts. I decided I would one day become a great golfer. And so, everything changed. Suddenly the club pro at my golf club approached me and encouraged me to start practicing on the range. He was patient with me and really got me going. I started to read golf magazines, interact with friends who are golfers, and ultimately gained a golf coach. Having avoided the club for so many years I really did not know anyone. But one day I was invited by two brothers to join them in their game. I warned them I was in the learning phases of the game. Despite how strong they were at the game, they had no problem with me joining them. They gave me tips and were very patient with me as I learned. Interestingly, many times we would end up at the club during the same hours, even though we had no prior plans.

As I focused more on golf, I was attracted to games with remarkably good golfers, one of them being a business partner of mine, Gary Hollister. What an honor to have one of my partners and mentors suddenly have me join his game with his circle of amazing golfers. (All of whom, may I add, were very patient and had no problem with me tagging along.) It's like the quote by Tony Robbins, "Where focus goes, energy flows." My focus had shifted and energy started flowing there. Suddenly I was attracting all sorts of golf into my life and although I have a long way to go, I am gradually improving and I am in love with the game.

So what happened? What was the difference? The difference is that I set my mind on golf, and with that focus I began to attract golf into my life. You may say, "Well, I do think about things, but they never come true." This is something that happens all the time. In fact, it is one of the things that causes people to throw up their hands and give up on the law of attraction. But the reason why this happens—the reason why results aren't what you think they should be—lies within you. Hold on and join me in Chapter 7: Dream for my discussion on faith and limiting beliefs. I will also discuss dreams and provide a method to help you reach your dreams.

There is Power in Thoughts and Words

More and more scientists and professionals are doing experiments on the law of attraction and proving it works. You may have heard of the Japanese scientist, Dr. Masaru Emoto, who performed studies on water and the freezing of water crystals. He states that our bodies are approximately 70 percent water and the earth is approximately 70 percent water. He set out through a series of scientific experiments to discover whether the words that we speak to ourselves and to one another, the thoughts that we think, written words and prayer have any effect for good or bad in our lives. The results were compelling.

Dr. Emoto found that when positive words such as "love" and "gratitude" were spoken while water was freezing, the water formed into beautifully shaped crystals. The opposite happened when negative words like "I hate you" or "you fool" were spoken. Then the water formed into very dark and creepy crystals. When he played positive classical music, crystals formed beautifully, but the opposite happened with harsh heavy metal music. He had prayers performed over water and observed a transformation similar to that from the previous experiments. I highly recommend his New York Times best-selling book, Hidden Messages in Water. Fascinating stuff, indeed.

I recently read a book called Power vs. Force by Dr. David Hawkins, a clinical psychiatrist. He states, "For as we know, if one holds a particular negative thought in mind, a very specific muscle will go weak; if one then replaces the thought with a positive idea, the same muscles will instantly go strong. The connection between the mind and the body is immediate, so the body's responses shift and change from instant to instant in response to ones train of thought and the associated emotions." Isn't it interesting that a positive thought will create strength, yet a negative thought creates weakness? This statement alone is enough to have me fill myself with positive thoughts each and every day. Why? I want to be strong in all the roles I play in my life.

The Placebo Effect

Did you know that the placebo effect is 33 percent effective? In other words, one-third of illnesses can be addressed through our thoughts and beliefs. (Note: it also depends on the illness. Some are affected more easily than others, such as headaches, low energy, arthritis and hot flashes.) The U.S. Department of Health reports that 50 percent of severely depressed people get better if they take an antidepressant. However, they also report that 32 percent get better if they take a placebo, commonly known as a sugar pill. Think about that. A person's condition can improve simply because they believe they are taking medicine, even if they aren't. (By no means am I proposing that all clinical depression can be cured by taking a sugar pill. I am not a doctor. I am simply making a point that our minds are powerful.)

The following statement regarding the placebo effect can be found on WebMD: "Research on the placebo effect has focused on the relationship of the mind and body. One of the most common theories is that the placebo effect is due to a person's expectations. If a person expects a pill to do something, then it's possible that the body's own chemistry can cause effects similar to what a medication might have caused. For instance, in one study, people were given a placebo and told it was a stimulant. After taking the pill, their pulse rate sped up, their blood pressure increased, and their reaction speeds improved. When people were given the same pill and told it was to help them get to sleep, they experienced the opposite effects. Experts say that there is a relationship between how strongly a person expects to have results and whether or not results occur. The stronger the feeling, the more likely it is that a person will experience positive effects. The same appears to be true for negative effects."

Clearly our minds and thoughts are very important. We have a 33 percent chance of healing simply because of what we think. I believe that through proper techniques and training, that the percentage could be much higher. Placebo studies have even been done on people during operations, which shows just how powerful the mind can be. Our thoughts, beliefs and minds are powerful and have capabilities that we don't fully comprehend. It is our responsibility to learn how to partner with our mind on our life-long journey of dreams, discovery, enlightenment, fulfillment and happiness.

Vibrations

The concept of a person possessing "vibrations" is very intriguing. We've all said something like, "She's got good vibes," or "I wasn't getting very good vibrations from that guy." You've probably at some point walked into a room and felt that something wasn't right. Or upon meeting someone for the first time, you probably felt like they were "off" or "on." These experiences point to the vibrations (and corresponding emotions) we emit and how we attract people with similar vibrations.

Allow me to dive a little deeper into the subject of vibrations. Albert Einstein taught that everything in life is vibration. What he meant is that although everything is a solid, a liquid or a gas, if you go to a subatomic level then the protons, neutrons, electrons, and even smaller particles such as quarks and neutrinos, are all vibrating.

They are in constant motion. Take a look at your thumb. What do you see? You will see skin, hair, nails, veins, wrinkles, the shape of bones (and maybe even a ring). Now if you were to take a look at your thumb on a deeper level, you would find that it is made up of trillions of cells. Each cell is composed of — are you ready — approximately 100 trillion atoms, which are made up of different electrons, neutrons and protons. These atomic particles are composed of subatomic particles such as quarks, all of which are vibrating.

They are in constant motion. Take a look at your hand. What do you see? You will see skin, hair, nails, veins, wrinkles, the shape of bones and possibly a ring or two. Now if you were to take a look at your hand on a deeper level, you would find that your hand is made up of trillions of cells. Each cell is composed of — are you ready — approximately 100 trillion atoms, which are made up of different electrons, neutrons and protons. These atomic particles are composed of subatomic particles such as quarks, all of which are vibrating.

Consider the possibility that with each of our bodies being a vibrational "universe," we have an ability with our thoughts and intentions to move subatomic particles, which in turn moves atoms, which in turn influences cells, which in turn shifts our chemistry, mood and the direction we on both short-term and long-term basis. In other words, we have the ability to "get our vibrations right."

As we begin to direct our vibrations in a certain direction — toward happiness or sadness, success or non-success, prosperity or poverty, gratitude or ingratitude, love or hate, we will then attract that which we are vibrating toward. As the old sayings go, "Like attracts like," or "Birds of a feather flock together."

In his book *The Science Behind the Secret: Decoding the Law of Attraction*, quantum scientist Travis Taylor explains: "But no matter what the reality is at any given instant, when you have a new thought, you are setting up a new quantum state. With each thought, a new qwiff is generated that begins interacting throughout the universe. Your new thought continues to interact with the universe and with the other qwiffs in the universe that are similar to it until a new entangled and common qwiff coheres and becomes the next instant reality. Napoleon Hill in his book, Think and Grow Rich states, "thoughts are things." They really are "things." I believe that thoughts are "vibratory things" and to me this really does explain so much of why we truly do go towards what we think about most.

As we get our vibrations right each day and keep vibrating at a higher level, we will over time be attracted to what we need and seek. This includes our dreams. For instance, if we want to lose weight or improve our health, we will be drawn to it rather than feel like it is simply a chore or duty. Pure foods with high vibrational energy will be attractive to you, and you will be drawn to such foods. Instead of having to force yourself to find and eat such foods, this attraction will happen naturally. It won't feel like a rule—rather, it will be a pleasure.

Music and Vibrations

Sound is a transfer of vibrations. Vibrations are created and transferred through a medium that is referred to as the "ether" and received by our ears and translated into sounds that we perceive to be words, basic sounds and music. These vibrations also evoke emotions within us.

Have you ever felt great, uplifted or happy while listening to a certain song or type of music? The opposite can also be true depending on how the music is arranged. You may have heard of studies demonstrating the effect of music on the growth of plants or how music being played to a baby while in the womb is beneficial. It's true. Music affects us. Take, for example, the belief regarding music's relationship to chakras.

First, I find it interesting that all music worldwide, no matter its origin or culture, is composed of seven notes—A, B, C, D E, F and G. Consider that numerous cultures and belief systems promote the existence of seven chakra points in the body (a chakra is defined as an energy channel that promotes balance and health).

In chakra teachings, each of the seven chakra points in our bodies are associated with one of these musical notes. Starting on the bottom chakra and going up to the crown chakra, they are as follows: Root - C, Sacral - D, Solar Plexus - E, Heart - F, Throat - G, Third Eye - A and Crown - B. Is it possible that the music we listen to has the capability to balance energy centers in the body?

If you are interested in trying to balance your energy centers, there is music created specifically to balance all seven chakras and once again can be found on YouTube. Or you can purchase different chakra balancing music from iTunes or on CDs. However you go about it, this is a powerful way to meditate and help a person become present and feel balanced. Is this a coincidence that the seven musical notes correlate to emotions and energy centers in our bodies? I don't think so. Once again, our bodies and spirits are a miracle.

Don't Complain

One other tip on how to keep our vibrations strong each day. I would like to propose one thing you can start doing today that will make a big difference—DON'T COMPLAIN!

First of all, no one likes to hear complaining from other people. It's "icky." There is a difference between complaining and constructive criticism. We do have to address issues within our relationships, work environment and other areas of our lives. Your inner guidance system will let you know the difference. If it's constructive, then approach it with love. If it is a complaint, simply don't go there. Resist the urge to complain.

Here's one example. I recently boarded a 6-hour flight after a demanding trip. I realized upon sitting down that there was no entertainment system in the plane. It was a small issue, I know, but I had been traveling all day and was ready to "decompress" a bit with a movie. I had a choice while talking with my wife during the boarding process whether I would complain or not. I decided to not say anything. What good would it do? She couldn't change it or magically make something appear. I couldn't do anything. Complaining would have only put me in a negative vibrational "funk." I ended up having an amazing flight, filled with solitude, peace and reading.

Ask yourself, "what good will it do me and those around me if I complain?" Remember, you are in charge of your vibrational pattern and your attitude, which will ultimately determine how your minutes, hours, days and weeks will go. Resist the urge to complain. Complaining does no good.

Conversely, constructive criticism, if done in the spirit of love, can be helpful. It says that you've identified a need to improve something and have come with a solution and a desire to improve that need. What if I wanted to help the airline understand my concern (which I didn't really -- it wasn't that big a deal to me, though to some it could be)? It would do no good to approach the airline attendant. She couldn't do anything. Maybe I could have taken the time later, and in the spirit of love, to write a letter to the airline company. Then I would feel better and possibly would be contributing to the solution rather than just being an annoyance to others around me. So, I invite you to get your "vibrations" right each day. Fill your mind with positive material. Do this through engaging in the "Take 5" regimen. Read and listen to audio books and podcasts. View positive social media and videos. Surround yourself with positive people, people who will encourage you to achieve your dreams, people who will lift you and not pull you down. Remind yourself daily of your blessings. Watch how this seemingly simple principle can begin a transformation that will take you to a whole new level. The power is within you. Tap into it. We need you strong. We need your dreams.

Laughter Truly Is Great Medicine

Laughter can have a transformative effect on your emotions and the situation you are experiencing. I believe laughter can help correct the vibrations of the mood from grumpy, anger, bitterness, frustration or whatever the negative emotion may be to happy vibrations. It breaks a pattern and helps you see a situation from a different perspective. My teenage son has a system of turning a bad mood

"For to no other creature, in the kingdom of our earthly mother, is given the power of thought. All the beasts that crawl and the birds that fly live not of their own thinking but of a law that governs all life. Only to the sons and daughters of men is given the power of thought and even that thought can break the bonds of death. Do not think because it cannot be seen that thought has no power. For I will tell you truly the lightning that cleaves the mighty oak, the quaking that opens up cracks in the earth these are the play of children compared to the power of your thought. Mankind has forgotten this power, for man does not see the world of the spirit."

Essenes, the Gospel of Peace

into a positive experience through laughter. He believes that a person cannot stay negative or mad at another person while listening to the song, "Monster Mash." So far it has been 100-percent effective for him. We use it in our household. We have had typical family moments where things are tense for one reason or another and he will play this song and it makes us laugh and the mood shifts almost immediately. It is so fun to watch firsthand. Laughter can truly change the vibrations from negative to positive. Try this or something else to create laughter and help break the pattern. It is not always this easy—but sometimes it is and it is right in our grasp if we want it.

CHAPTER 3

Gratitude

To make our life what we want it to be, we've got to work at putting "Positive IN." Gratitude is a perfect way to start putting positive into our minds each and every day.

What is gratitude? In the dictionary, gratitude is defined as, "The quality of being thankful; readiness to show appreciation for and to return kindness." It is interesting that gratitude has the ability, according to this definition, to pay it forward, "to return kindness." Gratitude could be defined as an emotion, or it could be an attitude. People often talk about an "attitude of gratitude." It rhymes and it is easy for us to understand. Gratitude also leads to faith. For me, gratitude is a key element to starting my day right and then keeping it going each and every day. Gratitude has an ability to transform a day from being mundane and insufficient to magical and abundant. Gratitude helps to bring life and this world we live in alive.

I love this quote from the book The Alchemist, "For her every day was the same. And when each day is the same as the next it's because people fail to recognize the good things that happen in their lives every day the sun rises."

What Is Gratitude?

Before getting into how to practice gratitude, I want to talk a little more about what it is.

Gratitude is finding the beauty in a sunny day. Gratitude is feeling the vitamin D from the sun enter your body and give you health and wellness. Gratitude is watching the sun rise in its glorious beauty and watching it set in awe. It is noticing the simple and complex life giving properties of the sun manifested all around.

Gratitude is greeting a rainy day with enthusiasm and excitement for what the rain will bring to your world around you. Watching the raindrops roll along a leaf. Watching the rain roll down a hill. Watch a child running in the rain. It is feeling the world around you soak in the life-giving properties of the moisture it so much needs for life to prosper.

Gratitude is finding the serenity in fresh snow that is falling. Instead of cursing the snow you welcome it, recognizing that somehow God in his infinite brilliance creates not one snowflake to be like another. This echoes the profoundness of the Zen saying, "Each snowflake falls in its appropriate place," reminding us that all is as it should be and to learn to grow from each and every moment of our lives. This also reminds us that we too as human being have been created different to one another and have purpose and are needed during this great journey on earth.

Gratitude welcomes spring for the flowers it will bring, the life that will come to your surrounding environment. Where people see brown, icky colors and mud and rain, you will see spring as a way to usher in new life and bring warmth to the land around you. You will watch the buds start on the trees and blossom into absolute beauty and abundance of life. You will smell the amazing sweet aroma of the lilacs and flowers that spring forth from this earth that we so easily forget is happening because it seems to do just that — "happen." Instead of being annoyed by the bees, gratitude encourages you to stop and watch in wonder at the miracle that is happening right before your eyes.

"Gratitude unlocks the fullness of life. It turns what we have into enough, and more. It turns denial into acceptance, chaos into order, confusion to clarity. It can turn a meal into a feast, a house into a home, a stranger into a friend. Gratitude makes sense of our past, brings peace for today, and creates a vision for tomorrow."

– Melodie Beattie

Gratitude does not curse the hot sun of the summer, but rather says thank you for the brief moments of the year (or possibly longer moments depending where you live) where the sun is so amazing and warm. Long summer nights when the sun stays higher in the sky longer than other times, offering more time to enjoy spending it with family and loved ones outside in mother nature's glory. It is expressing gratitude for amazing gifts, such as a tree that offers shade or the invention of air conditioning and fans that we have access to in this amazing world of progress.

Gratitude finds the greatness in the changing of the leaves and how they know when the time is right to change colors and fall from their branches. It is stopping and noticing the colors and recognizing the miracle that is taking place in the change of the season. It is enjoying the cultural experiences that come with each season of the year.

Gratitude is not being annoyed with the cry of a baby that is around you; rather, gratitude sees that baby as sounds of heaven. Gratitude truly can change our perspective, as what once was the cause of irritation is now the focus of our hearts. Reaching out and giving a helping hand to a mother who may be struggling in line and desiring to lighten her load.

Gratitude is leaving the days of irritability regarding traveling and finding the miracle and adventure that travel truly is. Instead of cursing yet another airplane, airport, hotel, traffic experience, bus or whatever the mode of transport is, gratitude helps us realize how much we have progressed in the past several hundred years and turns travel into an adventure. Gratitude turns a once-negative experience of waiting in a line to uttering the words, "Zippideedoo-dah—I now have time to get out my book that I have always wanted to find time to read and read a few pages." It takes this experience one step further and helps you realize how amazing technology is to allow us to hold volumes of books on the very device with which we make phone calls, send texts, send emails, Google information, look up directions, play games and listen to music.

Gratitude helps you find the good in other people. Gratitude helps you find the good in yourself and remind you of the miracle that you truly are. Gratitude is love. Gratitude is bliss. Gratitude is finding the good in the good and the good in the not so good in our lives. And in finding the good in the not so good, we recognize that within us is greatness and that greatness is manifested as we embrace the not-so-good moments and experiences and chose to grow and become the person we were meant to become.

Gratitude helps us recognize that the lonely moments in our lives as we endure through the not so good, define who we are and who we become, if we open up our heart and soul let them instruct us. Gratitude is transformational. Gratitude is a fundamental law of the universe and will put you into a vibrational pattern that can truly transform your life and help you grow, no matter what life sends your way.

Gratitude invites inspiration where you never thought inspiration was possible. Gratitude welcomes peace and harmony. Gratitude calms a troubled soul. Gratitude draws us closer and closer to the source of all that is good. Gratitude, my friend, will bring you to live every moment of every day. Gratitude will slow down time because you will notice what miracles surround you each and every moment of every day, from the sunrise to the sunset. And the most amazing thing about gratitude? It's free!

Gratitude is number one on my daily take 5 because gratitude puts our minds, hearts and bodies in the correct vibrational pattern by recognizing all the blessings we currently have in our daily lives and then moving forward in faith and belief toward a happy, healthy, productive day.

How can you practice gratitude each day? To begin with, take one minute to list that which you are grateful for. (As you make this a daily habit or ritual you will naturally go beyond one minute, but this is a good time frame with which to start. You may actually find yourself going beyond one minute as you begin this exercise.) This seems pretty straight forward and possibly too easy – and it is free. So how can it be so powerful? Exactly my point. It is free, it is simple, everyone can do it and it is transformational. You can do this in many different ways:

Music. This is not necessary for this experience but you may enjoy it. As I mentioned earlier, emotion associated with thoughts and dreams will help with lasting change. Music for me is a great way to couple emotion with gratitude. I like to use positive and peaceful music. You don't have to but I like it in my daily moments of quiet and reflecting. It will be different for each person. I have collected songs over time that I use for this process but much can be found for free on YouTube. Just type in a search for peaceful, relaxing or meditation music. There are so many options. Play the music while you are listing that for which you are grateful. Once you do this pause and think about how you feel. It is real.

List it on paper. Oprah Winfrey encourages a gratitude journal. This is an easy way to review that which you are grateful for each and every day. This is particularly powerful because it helps strengthen the connections with our body and mind by putting pen to paper. If this is the method you use be sure to do this first thing in the morning, again setting up your entire being to be receptive to inspiration, happiness and abundance.

Thought and meditation. Shut out distractions and put yourself in the present. This is particularly easy to do first thing in the morning before your daily routine gets too busy, as well before going to bed when naturally you should be relaxing your mind and body preparing to go to sleep. As you practice this daily, you will find that you can become present and quiet your mind even in busy environments. It will amaze you how healing and transformational a quick gratitude session can be for you even in a busy surrounding. If you are able to be completely still, close your eyes and take one minute to list that which you are grateful for. Good luck keeping it to one minute but again it is a good start. This can also be done while exercising or walking. I practice this while going for runs. I will stop for 1-5 minutes and just become still and give thanks for what I am experiencing. Powerful stuff indeed.

Prayer. Some people express gratitude in the form of a prayer. This is great and I encourage you to continue in prayer. However, I encourage you to be careful not to get into a rut saying the same things each day, trying to race through the motions of prayer. Doing so makes it so we don't actually recognize what we are saying, lessening the power of gratitude and prayer. I found myself experiencing this in my own life, which caused me to step back and truly look at what I was grateful for and why.

Dissecting Gratitude. There is power to not just listing something we are grateful for, but also discovering why we are grateful. Allow me to explain this with a story where I was reminded that our bodies are an absolute miracle. I love endurance sports. While training for an Ironman competition I spend a lot of time swimming, biking and running. Why? Because an iron man distance triathlon is a 2.4 mile swim, 112 mile bike ride, followed by a 26.2 mile run. Hence, training has a lot of swimming, biking, and running. I do much of my swimming at a local Olympic-size pool close to my house. It's a great place, but swimming back and forth, 50 meters each way, day after day can get quite boring and mundane. In fact, I was really just going through the motions of swimming – not really thinking about it much – until I had something profound happen to me.

I was behind another swimmer as we approached the wall in the deep end, just like I have done countless times over the years. In anticipation of reaching the wall, and in an attempt to avoid hitting the swimmer ahead of me, I found myself under water, watching him kick off the wall. As I watched, it was as if time stood still for a moment, as if the other swimmer were momentarily suspended under water. In that moment I was inspired to think of the miracle of the human body and what we experience each and every day. As I kept swimming I thought of what my body was going through to experience a seemingly mundane swim workout. I thought of my trillions of cells and how they communicate through my body to help me have that workout. I thought of my mind and all the signals it was sending throughout my body for my motor skills to happen. I thought about my lungs allowing much-needed oxygen to reach my body. I thought of the blood pumping through my system, starting with my heart and going through nearly 100,000 miles of arteries and veins and capillaries. I thought of my skin, liver, kidneys, stomach, and digestive system – every part of my body that was performing its incredible function to simply help me swim. And I realized that I was taking it all for granted. Suddenly my swim was no longer "boring", it was no longer "mundane." It became a miracle. I was reminded that I am a miracle, that we are all miracles and that what we experience each and every day is a miracle. You, my friend are a miracle. Much like with my act of swimming, you can experience this in your day-to-day activities. By way of exercise, I encourage you to implement this technique. Shut off your iPod on your next run for even 5 minutes of the run and start to express gratitude in your mind for what your body is experiencing to help you go through your run. Do this while walking. Do this while reading. Do this while eating. Do this before sleeping and recognize what a miracle sleep is in your life. Do this while your 5-year-old daughter busts into dance while walking through the mall and instead of wondering and worrying what everyone is thinking, marvel in the miracle that your daughter is to be able to accomplish that act from her mind to her actions. Become conscious the next time you turn on the lights and recognize what your body goes through to make that action happen. You, my friend, are a walking miracle.

What are you grateful for?

This list is truly endless, but may be difficult to begin creating. Once you get into this habit or ritual, you will find it opens a door to the amazing creation that you experience each and every day. Here are a few things for which you could consider being grateful:

1. You: May I propose you start with yourself. As I point out in the section on Love, it is hard to love others and treat others with respect if you don't love and appreciate yourself. As I mentioned in my earlier story, you are a miracle. Each one of us on this planet is unique and an absolute miracle.

2. Spouse or significant other: If you are married or in a relationship, express gratitude for that individual and list qualities that you admire and love about that person. This can be fun and possibly remind you why you fell in love with them in the first place, if that is needed. Include qualities, talents, abilities, things they do well, things they do for you that may have become daily acts of kindness but are now overlooked because it is just that—daily. Don't be afraid to include the qualities about their looks that you admire and love. What attracts you to them now, or what attracted you to them originally? Take your gratitude a step further from your lists and tell them. It just might end up nicely for you.

3. Children: Every parent can attest that each child is different and come to this world with a unique personality and set of talents. Take the time to list them. Remind yourself what you love about your children. By doing so you will find that you may stop focusing on their faults but rather their strengths. You will find possibly immediately and over time that your relationship will improve as you recognize the good in your family members rather than focusing on what is lacking.

4. Your food. You may be in the habit of saying a prayer over your food. This is great. However, as I mentioned with daily prayers, this can become the same words each time, thereby lessening the power of this experience. To help me truly appreciate the food that I eat I find myself going through an exercise of gratitude when approaching the food that I eat each day. Allow me to highlight an example of this. If you are like me, you have several favorite breakfasts. One of my "go-to" breakfasts is a particular shake. It is a vanilla/banana, peanut butter shake. I mix almond milk, vanilla protein, full banana, peanut butter, ice and honey. Sounds pretty basic correct? However, if you take a closer look at the shake and break it down, you will recognize that those ingredients do not magically appear at my house. The shake is the result of many companies who produce each of the products, a supply chain of trucks, depots, warehouses, forklifts, boxes, manufacturing facilities, growers of bananas, almonds, honey, store clerks who put the products on shelves, food agencies to ensure the food is safe for consumption, the companies that make the almond milk and the protein powder and the companies that produce the packaging and labels for each of the products. The list goes on and on. As you express gratitude for the shake, you will also feel gratitude for the job you have that supplies the money that enables you to go and purchase everything you need for the shake. Suddenly your simple breakfast turns into a miracle and true blessing. Whether through prayer or simply taking a moment in your mind and heart to express gratitude for your food, it will help take a daily experience that can be just a motion and turn it into a miracle and blessing.

5. Employment: As I mentioned in this past point, being grateful for the money you earn through your employment can be part of your daily gratitude session. I do propose that if you are not happy with your employment, daily gratitude for what it provides in your life will help you see it differently and make it more fulfilling. Your employment offers you the chance to make money that put food on your table, gas in your vehicle, clothes on your back, pay rent or mortgage, have family experiences (such as vacation), and so forth.

6. Be grateful for your dreams before they actually happen. In his book, The Science of Getting Rich, Wallace Wattles states the following: "Faith is born of gratitude. The grateful mind continually expects good things, and expectation becomes faith. The reaction of gratitude upon one's own mind produces faith; and every outgoing wave of grateful thanksgiving increases faith." You may be asking yourself what a chapter on gratitude and thanksgiving has any business being in a book about getting rich? It plays a big part in achieving your dreams, including seeking after wealth. In my daily gratitude, I give thanks for my dreams as if they have already happened. With this gratitude it requires true belief and faith in your dreams as well as patience. I will discuss this in further detail in the chapter about dreams so stay tuned. I have, however included it here at this point because it is a big part of helping our dreams to come true. Gratitude helps to set our mind, body and spirit in a vibrational pattern to prepare for dreaming. And if done correctly, it will naturally lead to action.

For example, if you want to achieve a certain weight loss goal, don't focus on "losing weight" because by doing so you are focusing on a negative. Rather, express gratitude for being perfectly healthy and having a body that is capable of miracles. Express gratitude for the weight goal that you are shooting for. If you weigh 150 pounds and you want to be 140 pounds, then give thanks that you are 140 pounds and healthy. You will find that you will be in the correct vibrational pattern and begin to "attract" 140 pounds. You will attract an action plan that will naturally take you to this weight goal. Of course, this requires an action plan that will include possibly a little more movement in the form of exercise or just becoming more active, some adjustments to eating patterns, better sleep, supplements, self control and willpower. But if you don't position your mind in the correct direction and maintain it, all of this is far too easy to fizzle out. It begins to feel like you're pushing a rock up a hill.

Here's another example. Try saying, "I am grateful for an abundance of happiness". But what if you are not happy? Express gratitude for being happy and watch how you will attract happiness in your daily life. It is moving forward in faith and belief. You likely won't experience an immediate result, but that's okay. Be patient. Becoming unhappy may have taken you years and even decades. I will assure you, your mind and body are miracles and can accomplish things very quickly if focused correctly. You have "learned" to be unhappy in your life. Therefore you can be "unlearned," and it starts with expressing gratitude for what you have, including being happy. Gratitude is a key part of our dreams coming true.

Are you looking for something else to be grateful for? Allow me to highlight a few things that I believe tend to be overlooked and possibly taken for granted. It may sound random, but that is the point.

The Earth

Consider the following about this amazing earth that we are blessed to experience each and every day. The earth spins at 1040 miles per hour. The earth is approximately 93 million miles from the sun. The earth travels approximately 1,599,825 miles per day. The earth and all of us on the earth are traveling 66,659 miles per hour. The sun is also moving through the universe at about 45,000 miles per hour. The moon orbits the earth at 2,288 miles per hour. What's amazing is that all these things are happening without us even knowing or recognizing they are happening. We can be grateful that gravity helps keep our solar system and our universe in order, grateful that the moon helps regulate our water tides. Isn't it wonderful that the sun's distance helps much of the earth experience the miracle of spring, summer, autumn and winter. What do each of these seasons mean to you? What joy do they bring you? What traditions come with these seasons that help bring happiness in your life?

Photosynthesis

The dictionary defines photosynthesis as "the complex process of which carbon dioxide (C02), water, and certain inorganic salts are converted into carbohydrates by green plants, algae, and certain bacteria, using energy from the sun and chlorophyll." Wow! This happens every day and we reap the benefits of this miracle, yet how often do we include this as part of our list of things to be thankful for?

Sunrise and Sunset

Every sunset or sunrise, unless we take the time to recognize them, will just be the same each and every day. But each is very different from the others. I love a sunrise and sunset. And they are different depending on the seasons. They are different depending on whether it is calm or windy. They are different whether it is raining or snowing, overcast or clear. I am blessed to have mountains both in the east and the west of where I live in Utah. Watching a sunrise or sunset with mountains can be a spiritual experience.

As I write this there is snow on the tops of our mountains, which seem to glow as the sun is setting. And it sets early this time of year. Sunsets with an ocean, lake, river or pond are also unique. Take a moment to stop and enjoy the experience and miracle that it is in your life each and every day and watch your love for life grow.

Wind

Wind can be annoying and, in extreme cases, destructive. However, for the daily winds that come into our lives, have you ever stopped to consider how important it really is? Wind can be very beautiful. Watching wind move through leaves and trees can create a sense of awe and wonder. Take a step further and listen to the wind move through leaves and trees.

"For her every day was the same. And when each day is the same as the next it is because people fail to recognize the good things that happen in their lives every day the sun rises."
– The Alchemist by Paulo Coelho

To get more technical, it's interesting to note that turbulence created by wind increases the CO_2 supply and so helps to increase photosynthesis. Gratitude for one thing can link to gratitude of another.

Bees

Bees are responsible for pollinating approximately one-third of our food supply and 90 percent of our wild plants and flowers. They go day in and day out doing their thing—yet do we really notice them? Let's be grateful for bees.

People

We all play many roles in society. We interact with each other on many different levels, whether as family, friends, neighbors, work associates, or people we come in contact with at stores, restaurants, gas stations, schools, and so forth. There are many opportunities every day to simply express thanks to others for whatever you have experienced in your interactions with them. It doesn't take much time but it just might help someone's day change for the better, starting with yourself. Here are some examples:

Store clerk – My father would quote Dale Carnegie to us and remind us that the most important sound in any language is the sound of a person's name. If the clerk is wearing a nametag, thank them for their good service and call them by name. If they are not wearing a nametag, ask them their name and then thank them.

Servers – Call them by name and thank them for their good service. If they do a good job, tip them and tell them why they made such an impact on your day. This is especially important in the United States, as servers get paid a very small wage and depend largely on tips to make their living.

Cooks and chefs – Cooks rarely get thanked. Why not take a moment to express thanks if the meal you had was enjoyable. It may not be appropriate to do in person depending on how busy it is, but something that works nicely is to buy the cook/chef a drink of some sort. Tell them it is from your table and tell them what you loved about the meal. This is their form of art and they take their food creation seriously. They will love to hear from you.

Police officers — Sometimes police officers get a bad rap. I have no doubt there are some bad police out there and the media likes to remind us of it anytime one of them represents this profession in a poor light. The truth is, however, there are bad people in every profession. To that point, I will say that police in the United States where I currently live and am a citizen, and those in my home country of Canada are for the large part very good people who risk their lives each day so we can have peace in our streets, towns, cities, states, provinces and countries. I have a brother-in-law who regularly misses family functions and holidays because he is out serving our community as a police officer. Stop and thank them. They are there to protect us and keep order.

Teachers – Teachers don't get paid a high salary and yet they have such an influence in our children's lives. They are there every day, teaching and guiding our children. Express your appreciation to them. It may blow their minds. You really want to blow a teacher's mind? Call a teacher from your past and thank them for the role they played in your life.

I had such a teacher from my elementary school days by the name of Mr. Bob Walkinshaw, aka "Sir". He did not teach us "what" to think but rather, "how" to think. I had moments over the years to express gratitude to him and made sure I did before he passed away. He was such a great man and his students who experienced his teaching methods will be forever better for it. My siblings and I are some of those students. He took school outside of the classroom and into nature. We would go for walks during certain lessons to not just teach but also show us what he was teaching. He set up a make-believe town where each student had roles to play from bankers to mayor. He would teach us how what we learned in class was truly applicable in the real world. Thank you, Sir, for all you taught me. Even in passing from this world to the next I know you can hear mine and others express our thanks to you.

Health – Research shows that having an attitude of gratitude helps us to be happier and overall healthier. In 2003, Robert A. Emmons of the University of California, Davis, and Michael E. McCullough of the University of Miami conducted a study titled, "Counting blessings verses burdens: An experimental investigation of gratitude and subjective well-being in daily life." The study found the following:

- "Gratitude is effective in increasing well-being as it builds psychological, social and spiritual resources."

- "The experience of gratitude, and the actions stimulated by it, build and strengthen social bonds and friendships. Moreover, encouraging people to focus on the benefits they have received from others leads them to feel loved and cared for by others." (citing Reynolds, 1983). "Therefore, gratitude appears to build friendships and other social bonds."

- "Gratitude, like other positive emotions, broadens the scope of cognition and enables flexible and creative thinking; it also facilitates coping with stress and adversity. (citing Aspinwall, 1998; Folkman and Moskowitz, 2000)

- "According to the broaden-and-build model, gratitude not only makes people feel good in the present, but it also increases the likelihood that people will function optimally and feel good in the future."

The simple act of expressing or showing gratitude can help us be better in all the roles that we play. Do you want to be a better spouse/partner, parent, child, student, sales person, teacher, manager, business owner, store clerk and overall human being? Begin by expressing gratitude daily for what you want, what you receive and what you experience in life. We all want to improve, which is fine. We need to move forward in life, but it starts with being grateful where you are and what brought you to this point.

Next, exercise faith in expressing gratitude for already being that person with the attributes you want. Express gratitude for the dreams you've already accomplished – it is already done in your mind. These dreams may not be realized for years to come, but that doesn't really matter. You are starting to move subatomic particles in your body, which can move atoms, which move cells, which will influence your mood and ultimately shape your future. You are preparing for it to happen and attracting it into your life.

I invite you to adopt a daily habit and ritual of gratitude. You will recognize that your life is truly abundant. You will begin to think in terms of abundance and by so doing so your faith and belief in yourself, your dreams, and others around you will increase. With increased faith will come new ideas, new ways of thinking and new-found success in problem solving.

As you make gratitude a daily part of your life, you will start to see opportunities where you did not previously see them. You will find an increase in compassion and love for yourself and those around you. You will find beauty in things that you walked by every day and never seemed to notice. You will find wonder in the moment you are in instead of being distracted by what you don't have or what you feel you need to do. You will find that healing your body and soul will come more easily. Your patience level will grow and improve over time. You will begin to make sense of whatever challenge(s) you may be experiencing; solutions will come more easily and you will learn how to grow from the experience. You will discover talents that you have left collecting dust, or that you may not have even noticed were there. You will discover blessings all around you that you never knew existed. You will find yourself falling in love with life again and start to see once again the beauty that life truly is.

Is this possibly what Jesus meant when he said, "Become like a little child," to find the wonder in everything around us? Welcome to the world of gratitude and the journey that you are meant to take and can take each and every day. Don't wait another moment. Thank you for reading this section. I am indeed grateful for you.

CHAPTER 4

What Is Love?

The higher you climb on your journey of growth and enlightenment, the more you'll realize that there is no room in your world for hate, and there is only room for love. Hate, impatience, an unwillingness to forgive, bitterness, anger, and unfair judgment all hinder your inner guidance system and your ability to receive inspiration.

Love, on the other hand, opens up your soul to receive the needed inspiration is waiting for you to help you further your progression. Just as importantly, love quiets your ego, which in turn quiets your need to be right (and the other person to be wrong). Imagine what that would do to your relationships with family, friends, colleagues and so forth. Love directs your day to attract that which you love and helps others feel the healing powers of love through you.

Love will direct you to forgive, starting with yourself and then naturally looking to forgive others. Love will help you see others through a no-judgment lens. Love helps calm your soul and makes sense of that which is happening in your life. Love will make you kinder. Love will help you be more patient with yourself and those around you. Do you ever say to yourself, "I wish I could be more patient" or "I wish I could be more kind" or "I wish I was not so judgmental?" Tune into the power of love each and every day and watch your patience, kindness, sincerity, desire for good and finding the good in life and in others grow. You will start to notice ways to serve this great world.

Was this love always there? Yes, but until you tune into the dial, so to speak, of your love each day, it is sometimes difficult to feel and see it. Much like gratitude, the more we are grateful, the more we love that which we are grateful for, the more we notice and become conscious of the greatness around us. Love will emanate from you and through you to the world around and will indeed affect the world you live in.

Additionally, as you activate the power of love that exists in you, you will see the world change for the better. You will be attracted to light and have light direct and feed your soul. You will take the light that comes from love to shine through the darker moments, embrace those moments and let them help you grow and become who you are meant to become and learn that which is to be learned. You will also use the light that will shine that much brighter to help you see what you're supposed to see. Your greater love will brighten your light to see more clearly. Do you want to see the world as a more peaceful place? Start with living in love each and every day. The world will begin to transform before your very eyes, because you will see with love instead of fear. Love always conquers fear. The two cannot exist together.

Start by Loving Yourself

Where do you start with greater love? Start with yourself. This is not egotistical but rather pure. How can you be expected to love your spouse or significant other, your children, your neighbor, your job, learning, your good times and your not-so-good times, and your parents and family members if you don't love yourself? You will always be in conflict if you don't start with pure self love.

For some this may come naturally and be an easy transition. But more likely than not, it will be challenging and will require patience and time. Start each day with telling yourself you love yourself. What is it that you love about yourself? Again, this is not meant to be boastful. Your inner guidance system will tell you whether it is pure or not. If you find a voice trying to tell you during this process that you are better than someone else, recognize this is your ego and it is not a pure self love. Self love does not elevate you above others. It does not make you feel better than someone else. Self love is pure recognizing your divine nature. Self love is healing and the more you practice this and feel, the more others will want to take part and want to know what you have. This is because you will connect more with the divine and with your inner light, which will cause your light to burn brighter and to be felt by others.

The act of loving yourself, those around you and life itself is a process. It doesn't happen overnight. It takes time. Life is a journey. Be patient and enjoy learning each step along the journey.

Love

To start seeing life and all it has to offer in a positive light doesn't happen overnight. Life itself often seems to be pulling us in a negative direction. "Take 5" helps counteract the negativity and begins to fill us with all things positive. The second step in "Take 5" is particularly important: Love. To have positivity in our lives, we need love. This chapter will discuss the power of love and what we can do to make it a meaningful part of our daily lives.

"Amor vincit omnia, et nos cedamus amori." In translation, *"Love conquers all things, so we too shall yield to love."*
– Roman poet Virgil

How Can We Lead Our lives with Love?

Start and end your day, following your minute (or more) of gratitude with listing that which you love in your life. It is important to use the words, "I love..." and then list the things you love. This can be linked with gratitude and you will see cross-over on your lists. That is okay. Make a list in a form that you are comfortable with, whether in the form of a journal or in the form of meditation, thought or prayer. You can also add music to this if you would like. This will be similar to your gratitude moments. Make note of how you feel. Change is starting.

The Power Of Love

I invite you to think back on a moment in time when you were feeling particularly low and someone you felt close to reached out and gave you a hug and told you all would be okay. On several occasions I have come home from a challenging day at work feeling tired, grumpy and with an overall cloudy mind. Simply put, my vibrations were off. My wife is the one who can detect my moods. When I've had a difficult day, it is not uncommon for her to simply hug me and tell me she loves me. In those moments, I feel something happening in my body. Something changes. It is as if negativity is being zapped from my body. Sometimes I even fight it because I just want to be grumpy, but it is hard to push away the power of love.

I have been fascinated over the years with the power of love and its ability to conquer. It is my belief that love is so powerful that it has the ability to change the chemistry in our bodies, literally transforming moods, emotions, thought patterns, and beliefs. Love speaks comfort and gives hope. Deepak Chopra refers to this as "moving molecules." Anita Moorjani, in her book Dying to be Me, describes a miraculous near-death-experience she had while fighting cancer that ravaged her body. She explains that while she was on the other side, before coming back into her physical body, she felt an indescribable feeling of love. Everything was love. She says that even the atoms and the subatomic particles are made up of love. I really enjoyed how she described this because to me it makes sense. We are love, and because of this our bodies, hearts, organs, cells and emotions all respond to love.

If love can have this effect—if love can truly conquer all as Virgil says—then I believe we must lead our lives in love. This chapter is dedicated to the unseen but very real power we call love.

The Power Of Words

In an earlier chapter I referenced a study by Dr. Emoto on water. What his study shows is that words and thoughts can affect how water transforms as it freezes. Positive words can create beautiful ice crystals, while negative or ugly words create crystals that are ugly and unappealing. One of the words Dr. Emoto used in his study was love. He spoke and wrote the word in many different languages on a container of water. The result was very beautiful. Dr. Emoto teaches that because our bodies are 70 percent water, we can effectively transform our lives through certain words and actions. His work is very thought provoking and I highly recommend you review it yourself. As Dr. Emoto shows, the power of words could be one of the reasons why we experience a change when we associate more closely with love. I have had many experiences in life where I have seen this transformation take place. When we lead with love there is a shift, as if on a cellular level, within our body, and things change for the better.

Research On Love

In 1988, Harvard University researchers David McClelland and Carol Kirshnit conducted a study on how merely watching an act of love and kindness can have an effect on the human body. The study is titled "The effect of motivational arousal through films on salivary immunoglobulin." The researchers had 132 students watch a 50-minute video of Mother Teresa showing acts of love and kindness to people on the streets of India. They tested each student's saliva before watching the film, when the film ended, and then 60 minutes after watching the video.

What the researchers found is that the test students' immunoglobulin A (s-IgA) had increased after they watched the movie. What is even more intriguing is that the levels stayed elevated up to 60 minutes after watching Mother Teresa's acts of kindness and love. Why are these results significant? Because immunoglobulin A plays a key role in our immune system. Here is what PubMed.gov has to say about the importance of immunoglobulin A: "The vast surfaces of the gastrointestinal, respiratory, and genitourinary tracts represent major sites of potential attack by invading micro-organisms. Immunoglobulin A (IgA), as the principal antibody class in the secretions that bathe these mucosal surfaces, acts as an important first line of defense."

In a nutshell, this study shows that just watching acts of kindness and love can improve our immune system for a time. So what might happen if we were actually participating in acts of kindness and love? How much more powerful would that be? People love to get involved in helping others, and doing so helps them to feel good. I believe that it is innate in humans to want to help other human beings. We are drawn to this. I recognize that life can be challenging and sometimes it seems like it's all we can do to just keep our heads above water. That is why I am inviting us all to apply love more in our lives. I am inviting us all to have a renewed love of life, starting with ourselves.

Most people in the world are familiar with the Golden Rule: "Do unto others as you would have them do unto you." We read the "do unto others" part, but possibly forget about the part that says, "as you would have them do unto you." This implies a need for self-love. You may say, "But isn't that selfish?" Not in the least, my friend. Somehow we learn in life that self-love is considered selfish. But that is not true. I believe that if we start with a healthy self-love then we will truly want to reach out and help our fellow humans as we love and help our own self. Each major religion talks about doing good to others. Consider the following similarities to the Golden Rule:

Christianity

"All things whatsoever ye would that men should do to you, do ye so to them; for this is the law and the prophets" (Matthew 7:12). Christ also states, "Love thy neighbor, as thyself." If we don't love ourselves, it implies it may be tough to truly love our neighbor.

Confucianism

"Do not do to others what you would not like yourself. Then there will be no resentment against you, either in the family or in the state." Analects 12:2

Buddhism

"Hurt not others in ways that you yourself would find hurtful."
Udana-Varga 5,1

Hinduism

"This is the sum of duty; do naught onto others what you would not have them do unto you." Mahabharata 5, 1517

Islam

"No one of you is a believer until he desires for his brother that which desires for himself." Sunnah

Judaism

"What is hateful to you, do not do to your fellowman. This is the entire law; all the rest is commentary." Talmud, Shabbat 3id

Taoism

"Regard your neighbor's gain as your gain, and your neighbor's loss as your own loss." Tai Shang Kan Yin P'ien

Zoroastrianism

"That nature alone is good which refrains from doing another whatsoever is not good for itself." Dadisten-I-dinik, 94, 5

It is interesting that each world religion highlighted above shares a similar message when it comes to love. Is it possible they teach the principle of love in such a similar way because love truly is a fundamental answer to a happier and more fulfilled life? If so, how do we live a life of love? How do we start each day with love? How do we lead with love? How can we harness this power of love?

Like all things, it is in the doing. As we show acts of love and kindness, this power will strengthen within us, helping us tap into the true power of love and fulfilling Virgil's statement that love truly can conquer all. How about telling a friend or loved one that you love and appreciate them? That may be uncomfortable at first but watch the magic happen. How long has it been since you said "I love you" to your spouse, your child, your parents, a close friend? You may say, "Well, we don't do that in our family." I am proposing that you make a change to that family tradition and actually say the words.

A love for life

Life is truly a miracle. I love to stop and observe what life has to offer. I live in the mountains of Utah and never cease to be amazed at the miracle of a sunset or sunrise. I love to get up early and watch the sunrise over the mountains. To watch a sunset in Utah is magical. I also love the transformation of winter to spring, with buds turning into leaves and blossoms that come out only once a year. Take a minute right now to consider where you live and what you love about it. Consider how life truly is a miracle. As you go through your gratitude sessions, list life as a wonder. I love to watch children playing. I love to watch their wonder for life—everything is exciting to them! List your life as a wonder and miracle. Start your day with love for life and watch healing take place in all areas of your life.

Hugs

Over the years, I have had the privilege of doing business in Mexico and one tradition I enjoy is the way they hug. They hug differently than what I am accustomed to—they hug heart to heart. As an outsider to their culture I have picked up on this and notice that it is a more meaningful hug. How about giving a friend or a loved one a hug? Maybe your response is, "We don't hug in our family," or "We're not the hugging type." You may think otherwise after hearing about the power of hugs.

What makes a hug so special? Let's start with the fact that hugs just make us feel good. Hugs from my wife, my parents and my children make me happy! I have experienced the same happiness with friends, family members and even strangers. (Although I suggest that before you hug a co-worker or a stranger you get their permission.) A good and meaningful hug can shift our subatomic particles, which in turn can alter the chemistry of our bodies to influence our moods and ultimately change our day, week, month and future. Remember that atoms can move around, which moves molecules, which moves cells, which has an effect on us physically, emotionally, spiritually and even psychologically. It is truly the butterfly effect and we are in complete control. How is this done? A recent article titled "7 Reasons Why We Should Be Giving More Hugs" explains: "When we embrace someone, oxytocin (also known as "the cuddle hormone") is released, making us feel all warm and fuzzy inside. The chemical has also been linked to social bonding. "Oxytocin is a neuropeptide, which basically promotes feelings of devotion, trust and bonding," DePauw University psychologist Matt Hertenstein told NPR. "It really lays the biological foundation and structure for connecting to other people."

NPR also reported that "when someone touches you, the sensation on your skin activates pressure receptors called Pacinian corpuscles, which then send signals to the vagus nerve, an area of the brain that is responsible for (among many things) lowering blood pressure." Another benefit of hugs is that when we embrace, we immediately reduce the amount of the stress hormone cortisol produced in our bodies. Hugs also help our bodies release tension and send calming messages to the brain. In a nutshell, hugs are good for your health. Hug more regularly and watch the chemistry in your body and soul react.

Love for your job

"Choose a job you love, and you will never work a day in your life."
– Confucius

We have all experienced doing business with someone who is in love with what they do. They have a certain spirit about them. People who love their jobs are stoked to be at work. They show it and anyone who works with them knows it. Does this mean that they will never have problems? No. No one is immune to challenges. But they love what they do so challenges become obstacles to overcome rather than bringing them down and destroying their day.

Let me share a story of this principle at work. There are many restaurants in the Salt Lake City area but one sticks out above the rest— it's called Valter's Osteria. My wife and I adore this restaurant. My partners and I also like to take our clients and sales leaders to this restaurant. It is owned and operated by Valter Nassi (hence the name), who is originally from Tuscany Italy. Valter's Osteria is very popular—people from all around are attracted to his restaurant.

Why? Obviously, the food is a big reason—it's absolutely fantastic. But there is something special about this restaurant that helps it stand above the rest. When discussing this with my close friend and business partner Aaron, he pointed out that it is because of love.

It's true. Valter simply loves people—he loves to serve people, he loves to put a smile on a person's face with his food, service and ambiance, and he simply loves what he does. It is said that one of the key ingredients in Italian cooking (or any favorite dish, for that matter) is love.

This principle is very evident at Valter's Osteria. People are attracted to this business not just because the food is outrageously good but because they feel the heart of Valter and his staff when entering the restaurant. They feel loved, welcomed and wanted.

Does Valter have challenges? I am sure he does. But no one would know because his love for what he does surpasses whatever may come his way. He leads his business with love. Conversely, if you seek to lead with love in your work and business, you will never work another day in your life.

You may know people who simply are not happy with their job. In many cases they are miserable and it shows in their face and in their actions. Maybe you are not happy in your job. Maybe you are reading this and thinking to yourself, "But I have tried multiple jobs in multiple lines of work and they are all horrible." Maybe it was your boss or possibly the people you worked with; maybe it was the job itself. In some cases a change is needed. However, in more cases than not, an attitude shift is what may be necessary. Try to see your job as one you love. Find the good in it. How is it making the world a better place? Who benefits from your work? How does your product or service help a person in their day-to-day life? Find the good in your co-workers and in your boss. Maybe by seeking to understand them more you will find they are not so bad after all.

Earl Nightingale said, "Attitude is not the result of success. Success is the result of attitude." This true statement applies to how you see your work, employment and career. This can also go back to your gratitude sessions each and every day. What sorts of blessings do you have in your life and in the lives of those you may support because of your employment? Sometimes there needs to be a shift in attitude to make a world of difference.

If you are a salesperson, you are probably familiar with Og Mandino. In his worldwide bestseller, The Greatest Salesman in the World, he states that a salesperson who wants to be successful should say, "I will greet this day with love in my heart." He goes on to explain, "For this is the greatest secret of success in all ventures. Muscle can split a shield and even destroy life but only the unseen power of love can open the hearts of men and until I master this art I will remain no more than a peddler in the marketplace."

Be grateful for your employment and find a way to fall in love with what you do. Watch your interactions with your fellow employees change. Watch your interactions with your customers improve. You will find yourself with a new spring in your step as you approach your employment each day. Transformation will slowly but surely take place, though it will take work on your part. Shifting attitudes is not easily done, but you can do it. You have it within yourself to make this change.

Pay it Forward

Early in our marriage, my wife and I were celebrating some special event by going out to dinner. It was a beautiful restaurant, probably out of our price range, but we were there to celebrate and enjoyed the experience. We sparked up a conversation with the couple next to us who were in a different stage in life. They were much more mature and had experienced much more of life than we had at that time. At the end of our dinner and conversation, the couple announced to us that our dinner was their treat and that we were not to challenge them on it. They had one stipulation: we needed to do something similar to someone in the future. We graciously accepted their challenge and went away feeling very touched and blessed. That night our chemistry was shifted, and we desired to work hard in life so that we could bless others during their life journey.

There was a movie released in October 2000 titled Pay It Forward. It is about a student who creates a movement of doing good for others and how it continues on. Anyone who has seen this film will remember it is a beautiful story. You may have used the words "pay it forward" before. But does the concept really work? In the article "The Science of Paying it Forward," Melina Tsvetkova and Michael Macy relate a story of a person at a drive-through in Canada who paid for their food and then offered to pay for the person behind them. That person then did the same and the chain continued for next 226 customers. I had a similar experience. A co-worker inspired me by performing this same act of kindness. There happened to not be anyone in line behind me so I gave the cashier at the window some extra cash and asked if she would be willing to do this for me. She graciously accepted and said that it is not uncommon that when this happens, the next person will then do it and so on and so on. Just as I was inspired by my co-worker, many other people have been inspired to pay it forward.

Paying it forward does not always need to be in the form of money. There are many things we can do to help make someone's day brighter. Some examples: You could randomly show up to help someone who needs to get work done on a project. You could stand up for someone at school or work who is being bullied. You could deliver a thank-you note to someone who has made an impact in your life. You could listen to someone who needs a listening ear. Much like the example of the drive-through, your good acts will inspire others to do the same and by so doing make the world a better place.

Smile

Smiling is a great way to spread a little love and brighten someone's day, starting with your own. And it does not cost one dime. Did you know that smiles are contagious? When you smile at someone, in almost all cases they will smile back. There is a connection from one human being to another. These connections are very real and they help improve our day. Have you ever experienced that moment when someone took the time to simply smile at you and it turned your day around? I have and I love it. I especially appreciate those amazingly beautiful smiles that some people have that are so sincere and show their absolute love for life.

When you share a smile with someone, take it one step further and ask them how their day is going. Look at them and with a sincere smile say, "How are you today?" Watch their day brighten. If they are with a group, smile and say hello to the whole group. It is therapeutic. Smiles make the world a better place. The world needs more smiles.

Love for Family Members

Loving our family members should be standard operating procedure for us all, but the ones closest to us often tend to be neglected. Don't let another day go by without saying in words and in actions how much you appreciate and love your family—especially a spouse or significant other and children. I promise you that there will be a change in the spirit of your home. Chemistry will be changing all over the place. Instead of starting your day arguing over the toothpaste or who will take out the trash, or wishing your child would not wear their hair in that manner (or those clothes or whatever it may be), start your day by placing your family at the top of your "gratitude list" and give them a big hug and tell them you love and appreciate them. Send them to work or school with a feeling of love and acceptance. Get their vibrations right as they leave the home. This will not only help them in their day but it will make a difference in yours.

As you express love and appreciation for your loved ones you will begin noticing the things that your spouse or significant other, your children, or your parents do daily that may have gone unnoticed or were not really appreciated. You will start to see more clearly. With love, the world begins to be a different place. Love for your family members and loved ones can transform relationships and break down barriers. Walls will come down, sometimes immediately, and sometimes more slowly. But love in a family will conquer all. Love will lead us to say "I am sorry" more quickly and lead us to forgive more readily. Two three-word sentences can change your home and begin to make the world a better place: "I love you" and "I am sorry." Yes, discipline needs to take place and disagreements will happen. That is normal and that is part of life. However, if things are done in a spirit of love it is very different from a spirit of anger. We have all experienced both and there is a difference. You can feel the difference. Anger makes us say things we wish we had never said. I find that when I approach family experiences with love and seeking to understand, it always works out for the best.

Send love to another human being

The HeartMath Research Center asks the following questions: "Did you know that your heart emits electromagnetic fields that change according to your emotions? And did you know that your heart's magnetic field can be measured up to several feet away from your body?" Rolin McCratey, Ph.D. Director of Research at the HeartMath Institute, explains, "By learning to shift our emotions, we are changing the information coded into the magnetic fields that are radiated by the heart, and that can impact those around us. We are fundamentally and deeply connected with each other and the planet itself."

This is a fascinating finding and explains much of what we experience when someone gives us a hug or passes on positive emotions to us in the form of a smile or by simply sitting and listening. Sending love to another human being can be done without the other person really knowing it, but they will feel it. This is a practice that could apply to a friend, a neighbor, a work associate, a client, a sales contact or a random stranger who could use some extra love. Out of these examples, consider the person you come in contact with who is having a particularly bad day and it shows. You may not know them but it shows and is felt in their countenance. Their vibrations are very negative and people around them who come in contact can sense it. Think about a person working in a restaurant or at a cash register or at security at an airport. If you can sense they are in a bad mood, while you are in line waiting, concentrate on that individual's heart and emotions. Pass emotions of love and compassion to that human being from one heart to another. Feel those electromagnetic waves pass from your heart to theirs. And move on with your life knowing that you have affected their emotions, even if just by a little bit. Passing on love and compassion will brighten your day and it can only make their day better.

Prayer and meditation

Consider the heart-to-heart connection we can have with other people and how that relates to prayer and/or meditation. Imagine if your prayers and/or meditation focused on the good of another individual or group of people. Now imagine multiple people, whether it be two or ten or a hundred or a thousand, praying and meditating with a focus for a good outcome for another human being or group of people. How powerful this can be! A great example of this happened in 1993 in Washington, D.C. There was a carefully controlled scientific demonstration by a group whose goal was to reduce violent crime. From June to July, people gathered in Washington D.C. to meditate for peace in the Washington D.C. area. Their intent and focus was to reduce crime by 20 percent. The Chief of Police stated that the only thing that could possibly drop crime by 20 percent would be 20 inches of snow during the summer month of June.

During the first week of the study, 800 people were meditating together. By the last two weeks of the study, 4,000 people were meditating. During that period of time, violent crime in D.C. dropped by 23.3 percent. That is statistically significant. Interestingly, when the focus and meditation stopped, crime increased again. Clearly something magical took place between June 7 and July 30, 1993. (See http://www.worldpeacegroup.org/washington_crime_study.html.) Miracles do occur in this world. Prayer and meditation are an absolutely powerful force for good in the world. I propose that we do not use this power enough. If we used prayer and meditation more as a force for good in the world, we would have a much more peaceful world, beginning with ourselves.

Gossip: Don't Do It

Simply put, if you are striving to grow and become enlightened in your life, there is no room for gossip. Gossip is poison to everyone involved, and it dims our 'inner guidance" system. In his book The Four Agreements, Don Miguel Ruiz states that gossip is like black magic. When we share gossip, it is like putting a hex on that person and it follows them. What does he mean by this? Gossip is defined as, "Casual or unconstrained conversation or reports about other people, typically involving details that are not confirmed as being true." That about sums it up.

Consider how much we are taught to gossip. The media is weighted heavily on gossip and casting judgment. The tabloids love to gossip about people and then lead us to have a certain opinion about a person, group of people, product/brand or organization. We often start our days watching or reading gossip in the news and then perpetuate it at work and with our friends and family. This is poison. Much of it is not even true. Then we continue this behavior with our friends, family, neighbors, work associates, church members and communities in general.

If you want to eliminate the effects of gossip from your life, a great rule is to simply stop it. My good friend and business partner Beverly Hollister has a practice of just saying, "Stop it." There is no room for this in our lives if we want to lead a positive life. Imagine if we could operate knowing that friends would come straight to us if there was a concern that they may have or question regarding something we did? Imagine if in relationships, each side could trust entirely that the other side is not gossiping to friends and family members about concerns that come up within the relationship? Trust builds confidence and stronger relationships.

So why do we gossip? It is my opinion that we do it to elevate ourselves over someone else in order to somehow cover up a feeling of insignificance or something missing in our own lives. Gossip tends to go hand-in-hand with casting judgment. I am not referring to making a judgment call on whether or not you go take candy from a stranger in an overcoat. I am referring to casting judgment on a person from what they may be going through. It is easy to make a judgment behind someone's back or even in person without knowing truly what that person is going through and what led them to make the decision they did or why they are in that situation. Mother Teresa said, "If you judge people, you have no time to love them". So very true. The Dalai Lama stated, "What is love? Love is the absence of judgment." Very similar statement to Mother Teresa. And Jesus stated, "Judge not, that ye be not judged. For with what judgment ye judge, ye shall be judged." If we spoke about people as if they were in our presence then we would speak very differently. If we look at a person with pure love we will look at the with non-judgment and see them as a fellow human being working their way through this amazing journey of life. If we are to lead in love we must shed gossip and judgment in our lives.

Give of your money

There is a truth in life that we need to learn in order to be happy. It is this: Whatever we want in life, we must be willing to give up. I discussed this in an earlier chapter. If you want love, you must give love without expectation. If you want money, you must give money without expectation of return. You may have heard this referred to as "karma", or "you reap what you sow." Many of us are familiar with the law of tithing. This is a more structured practice among Judeo-Christians where you give up to one-tenth of your earnings to charity. Islam calls it "zakat," or alms giving.

The idea of giving is not just a religious practice. Robert Kiyosaki talks about it freely in his books on wealth generation. Dr. Deepak Chopra discusses it as a law in life. Thomas Stanley and William Danko also talk about it in their 1996 New York Times bestseller "The Millionaire Next Door." They studied millionaires throughout the U.S. and found that the average millionaire gives a meaningful percentage of their income to charities. However you look at this practice of giving, I do believe that a key is not to give so that you can receive, but rather to give without expectation of money in return. By doing so you are helping people in ways that may never be known to you, but in return, God or the universe (however you want to look at it) will return the blessings. Test it out. It works. Make the world a better place.

Love conquers all

Start today being aware of and increasing love for yourself, for your family, for life, for your career, for schooling, and for those around you. Watch the changes that occur as the emotion of love permeates through all the roles that you play in life. As stated earlier, you will make the world a better place, starting with you. I believe that Virgil was right when he wrote those simple, yet profound words: "Love conquers all things, so we too shall yield to love."

CHAPTER 5

Be in the Moment

As we fill our minds and hearts with positivity, our outlook and desires will change and, as a result, our lives will change. To help with putting positive in, be sure to "Take 5" daily. "Take 5" refers to five things we can do to increase our positivity:

1) Gratitude

2) Love

3) Be in the Moment

4) Read

5) Dream

The previous two chapters looked at Gratitude and Love. This chapter will focus on the third part: Be in the Moment. Learning to quiet your mind will help you be in the moment and appreciate your life as it unfolds in the present.

Be Present

Life can be crazy busy. It is hard to truly be in the moment in our modern life. We seem to be connected at all times in the day. Let's take for instance our mobile phones. We text while we are eating. We text while we are walking. We text and check email while we are talking to other people. We check our twitter feed in the bathroom. We are often so busy that it seems we cannot do one thing at a time. We eat while we are at our desk. We eat while we are driving. We eat while we are walking because we are in a hurry. We eat while watching TV. We have dinner as a family and each person has their head buried in their phone, laptop or video game. We can't even watch TV without multi-tasking. We are trying to watch the show and ads are popping up, drawing our attention away from what we are watching. We watch the news and forget what we are watching as updates and newsflashes constantly stream across the screen. Watch sports and it is even worse. I am not sure if I am watching the updates on the MLB, NBA, NHL or all three at once. While I am trying to follow whatever story they are telling, my eyes and mind are drawn to the game scores at the bottom and highlights that are streaming at the side. It is information overload. Do we ever truly get in the moment? I have been guilty as the next person with this. Our world is full of information overload and it can be quite overwhelming.

There has never been a more important time than now to be present. To be present means to embrace the moment while shutting out distractions. To be present means to be aware of and focus on what is happening right now. The more we can become present, the more we can focus our energy and live life to the fullest. Think about it—the past is past; it's gone, never to be had again. The future has not yet arrived. When we spend our time in the present worrying about the past or the future, we waste that moment in time. As we become more present in our lives we recognize the wonder and miracle that life is.

A big part of being present is learning to quiet our minds. As we quiet our minds and stop the internal constant chatter, we open up our minds and our hearts to inspiration for all the roles we play in our lives. We activate the relaxation response in our body. In her book Mind over Medicine, Dr. Lissa Rankin states, "When the relaxation response is induced, the parasympathetic nervous system is in the driver's seat. Only in this relaxed state can the body's natural self-repair mechanisms go about the business of repairing what gets out of whack in the body, the way the body is designed. The relaxation response also improves mood. It is hard to feel anxious or depressed when the parasympathetic nervous system is in charge." In such a relaxed and positive state, life slows down, and as it slows we can hear things and feel impressions that we may not normally have heard or felt. We can get ideas and have inspiration. We can heal.

So how can you quiet your mind? Here's one simple way: Try to focus on your breathing for one minute. One minute is all you need to start with. This may seem simple—too simple. But believe it or not, you may find this to be tough. Again, our minds are perpetually racing, especially with our world of technology today. Start with one minute. Once you are able to do this, you will find it to be quite healing and will want to go longer. You will also learn that you can do this at different times during the day. It could be while at work when you need a quick "pick me up," or while standing in line at a store. I have practiced this while waiting at a ski resort. Kind of random, I know, but if you find yourself with some time, don't hesitate to practice this and feel of the power of becoming present. It is during this space between thoughts that inspiration comes. You will find patience comes a little easier. You will find ideas will begin to flow more. You will see a situation that may be challenging a littler clearer. Peace can be found with whatever it is you may be experiencing. You will begin to listen a little more. You will hear things you have not heard before. You will find yourself closer to your inner guidance system, opening up to ideas and thoughts. You will renew and rejuvenate faster. You will become more calm, cool and collected. Your health will begin to improve. The more you learn this and apply it in your life, the more peace you will feel.

I find so much peace from this that one minute is not enough, but it is a great starting point. As we learn to quiet the internal chatter of our mind and world, we open ourselves up to inspiration meant for us in our lives. In stillness, you will find that answers come easier in your life. I am not saying they will come immediately (although sometimes that happens). What I am saying is you are setting your mind, spirit and body into a vibrational pattern that is open to such inspiration.

Some people like to have music to help with this process. Some prefer not. I don't think there is a right or wrong answer here. When starting out, I do recommend a form of music. I personally love to use music in my life. There are so many meditation music options for free on YouTube or to be downloaded or purchased in the form of CDs. I find it to be very calming and soothing and helps me to quiet my mind, opening myself up for direction meant for me in my life. There is a reason why so many sages from the beginning of time tells us to turn within for answers. They are essentially saying to quiet your mind and look inside you. As Eckhart Tolle says, "Stillness speaks." The crazy thing is, it's free and it has always been there it simply needs to be activated. So tap into the source and begin to find yourself.

I want to now share five ways that in your life can help you be present and in the moment:

1) Stop worrying about the past

2) Enjoy your moment

3) Be in nature and connect with Mother Earth

4) Become silent and be still

5) Do something random

Stop Worrying About the Past

Have you ever seen the movie Napoleon Dynamite? Seriously funny movie if you like that sort of humor, which I do. Everyone laughs at Uncle Rico, who lives in his van in a farmer's field and is stuck living in the past. He is stuck dreaming of what his life would have and should have been had his coach played him in that one important football game in high school. He is literally playing the same story over and over. He even practices football and records himself on videotapes. It is funny. However, the sad reality is many of us do this in a lot of different ways. Are you stuck in the past with a relationship? A job that went sour? A friend who wronged you?

How about an investment that went south and you lost money? An accident that left you with health challenges? Do you have a family member who stopped speaking to you and you don't know why, so you constantly replay in your mind what you could have done differently? How about a dumb decision you made as a teenager that hurt another person's feelings and you can't seem to let it go? Were you bullied in junior high or high school and those emotions keep coming back? All too often we hit the replay button over and over and we just keep watching these moments of hurt in our lives. If it is not a replay button, then we are allowing the voices in our heads to talk this over and over and over. It is like we have an open wound on our hand and we keep cutting at it.

I know the past can be a painful place. We all have things we wish had never happened. In some instances we may need professional help to work things out. But we all need to get to a point where we stop worrying about the past. The past is the past and there is no amount of worrying and stress that can change it. I know this is easier said than done. But if you want to truly heal, you must let go of the past. Stop reliving it. I have heard of people putting a rubber band on their wrist and when they start playing the same images and conversations in their mind they snap their wrist with the rubber band to remind them to stop. Other people, when they start replaying the past, simply say, "Stop it," or "Enough."

If you start worrying and stressing about the past, ask yourself, "What does this do for me? Will it change the past? Will the worrying change the outcome of the past? Will the worrying and constantly talking and complaining about change anything?" Of course the answer is, "Not in the slightest bit." In fact, worrying and stressing will make it worse because now you are triggering a stress response. This means stress hormones rise in your body and this can be harmful to your health. Stress is the silent killer. How much undue stress do we cause ourselves each and every day because we keep reliving the past? And what is so sad is that all the time we are worrying about the past, causing harm to our bodies and souls due to the stress we are bringing on, we are missing our present. And the present is all we really have. Indeed, we need to spend our time in the present and make decisions in the present so we can be happy in the moment and have a hope for a better future. Stop worrying about your past. Do whatever you need to do to just let it go and enjoy your present life. Take a deep breath and make a commitment that your present will no longer be robbed by worrying about your past. It is a liberating feeling, is it not? So much peace can be found in just this one principle.

Enjoy your moment

Our lives are so full and so busy, we tend to not focus on what we are doing in the present; rather we focus on what the next activity is. We often tend to already be in the next activity before the first is complete. How often do we limit our enjoyment of a trip, date night, holiday, or season (like Thanksgiving) because we're already focused on the next trip, date night, holiday or season? And when we get to Christmas, are we already starting to worry about the bills that will come in, which further taints our present moment? How can we fully appreciate the present if our heads are in the future or worried about the past? Once again, what good does it do? I say to you, not one bit of good. We are watching life pass us by at warp speed rather than soaking in the present experiences. Time will slow down and your life will be more fulfilling if you stop and smell the roses, so to speak.

I had a beautiful experience recently while going for a walk with my young daughter. Going for a walk is one of the simple things she loves to do with our family, and I have learned to embrace these moments and enjoy them. Seeing the world from the eyes of a child is therapeutic in and of itself. While recently walking she pulled leaves from two different trees. Both of the trees were maple, but the leaves were different sizes. She held them up next to one another and pointed out that each leaf was the same but different sizes. I took the time to actually stare at the leaves and wonder at their beauty. These two simple leaves were fulfilling their role in life. Could this be what Jesus Christ mean when he said, "Consider the lilies how they grow: they toil not, they spin not and yet I say unto you, that Solomon in all his glory was not arrayed like one of these." The leaves are present. All flowers are present and so peaceful. Could this be why we have the saying, "Stop and smell the roses"? Do you get so busy in life that seasons pass and you take no notice of the miracle that has transformed your landscape? Would you like to recapture the feelings of wonder that you once had in your youth? Go out and just sit and observe. Observe the bee as it goes from flower to flower, just making things happen so we can have beauty all around and so that we can have honey. Observe the clouds move through the sky. Observe the colors around you—the many shades of green, the grays and blues, the variety of colors at different times of day and different seasons of the year. Stop and observe and enjoy whatever you are doing.

Be in nature and connect with Mother Earth

"Stop and smell the roses" naturally feeds into this principle. Turn off your phone and go for a walk or hike or run in nature. Turning off your phone is key. If you are checking your phone, you are allowing distractions that keep you from the healing that being in nature has to offer. I love to run on trails. I love to disappear into the mountains where I live. The further I go the quieter the sounds of the city get. I generally run the same trails over and over. However, recently I had a great experience when my second son my second son Ethan invited me to go for a run. He took me to a ski resort called The Canyons, which is located in the Park City area. I know the mountain there from a ski perspective, but I had never experienced the higher elevations without snow. He had us go straight up to the top of The Canyons resort, an elevation of around 10,000 feet. We then ran along the ridgeline to Park City. I was in awe. I could see as far as the eye would allow. We watched a rainstorm approach and barely miss us. We could see ski lifts and part of Little Cottonwood canyon on the other side of the mountain range. When we arrived at the top of Park City, I was able to see Jupiter ski lift with no snow and the lake that is always covered in snow and ice. We then worked our way down the mountain. It was an incredible experience. My phone was off. I didn't listen to music. It was just nature, and it was so healing.

Why is being in nature so good for us? One reason is vitamin D. In the article, "The Truth about Vitamin D: Why You Need Vitamin D," Daniel DeNoon states, "Your body must have vitamin D to absorb calcium and promote bone growth." He continues, "Vitamin D deficiency has now been linked to breast cancer, colon cancer, prostate cancer, heart disease, depression, weight gain, and other maladies." It is vital to our health and wellness. And our bodies get it by exposure to sunlight. In the August 2013 Life Extensions magazine we learn that "64 percent of Americans don't have enough vitamin D to keep all of their tissues operating at peak capacity." It is interesting how we have demonized the sun over the years. I propose we need to start inviting the sun back into our lives.

Another reason to go into nature and be active is to activate the endorphins in your body. In a Web MD article titled "Exercise and Depression" it states, "When you exercise, your body releases chemicals called endorphins. These endorphins interact with the receptors in your brain that reduce your perception of pain. Endorphins also trigger a positive feeling in the body similar to morphine. For example, the feeling that follows a run or a workout is often described as 'euphoric.' This feeling is known as a 'runner's high' and can be accompanied by a positive and energizing outlook on life." May I add that it doesn't have to be exercise or running that can help release endorphins. A good walk can also do this. Hiking is another amazing way to connect with nature. The point is that we are already hardwired to create euphoric feelings, peaceful feelings, feelings of being on top of the world. We just need to learn how to tap into it.

Would you like to take your outdoor experience to a different level? Consider walking barefoot. I know this may sound "hippy," but it is an amazing way to connect with nature and to the earth. My son Ethan is known to be barefoot wherever he goes. He loves being barefoot. I too enjoy it. I have found as I travel that if I go barefoot when I arrive, particularly if I have time zones to cross, I am able to overcome jetlag much more quickly. Why would this be? Dr. Mercola explains in an article titled, "Grounding: the potent antioxidant that few people know about…and it's free." He says, "The technique of grounding, also known as earthing, is simple: you walk barefoot to ground with the earth. The scientific theory behind the health benefits seen from this simple practice is that your body absorbs negative electrons from the earth through the soles of your feet. The earth is negatively charged, so when you ground, you're connecting your body to a negatively charged supply of energy. And since the earth has a greater negative charge than your body, you end up absorbing electrons from it. The grounding effect is, in my understanding, one of the most potent antioxidants we know of and may have an anti-inflammatory effect on your body." It is amazing. I invite you to try it. Get in the moment.

Become silent and be still

"There are strange moments in life when the mind rests without any kind of worries. When our mind is quiet, when our mind is in silence, then the new arrives." — Samael Aun Weor

As we become still, we are able to connect to our divine self, find inspiration, achieve peace of mind, find answers to life's challenges and learn to heal by shedding old habits of negativity, fear and anxiety. Consider the movement of yoga. Why is it that in our very busy world yoga studios are popping up everywhere? Along with yoga studios there are meditation sessions available for people to join. Why is this? One of the purposes of yoga it is learn to quiet the mind. It is my belief that as our lives become increasingly busier we are drawn to find ways of quieting our minds. We instinctively know this is necessary for our health and wellness, not just physically, but mentally, spiritually and emotionally.

In his book The Art of Smart Thinking, James Hardt, Ph.D., explains that alpha brain waves are responsible for our creative thoughts. We activate our alpha brain waves when we are not quite asleep, but also not quite awake. He states that we need to learn how to stop thinking in order to tap into our alpha or creative brain inspiration. It is our beta mind, or our thinking mind, that we use during most of our waking moments. Beta brain waves are problem-solving brain waves. When we are fully asleep we activate our delta brain waves. But, when we wake up and go immediately into problem-solving mode by going straight to emails, texts, work and stressing about what is in the news and life in general, we are back to beta thinking.

The more we can learn to quiet our minds through different techniques such as meditation, yoga or simply "chill" time, the sooner we can become strategic at tapping into our creative side of our mind and seeking the inspiration that we all have a right to as human beings.

EGO

I once heard the late Dr. Wayne Dyer say that the word ego stands for "Edging God Out." I like that. Our ego can very easily get in our way. Ego threatens our ability to learn from the inner voice that exists in us all. The more we quiet our minds, the more we humble ourselves in silence and the more our inner light can speak peace and give us knowledge and guidance.

The bottom line is this: there is power in quieting your mind. Inspiration comes, and your life will improve for the better the more you learn how to daily quiet your mind.

Do something random

Our lives are busy. We tend to get into a rhythm and do the same things over and over again. I like to try and do something random to break that rhythm and to become present. Let me give you an example. I had an experience once where my daughter, who was maybe three years old at the time, was getting out of my car in the garage. It was raining outside, one of those warm kind of rainy days. She instinctively ran outside on the driveway and started dancing in the rain. I said something like, "Hey baby, come inside, it's raining." Her answer was, "Daddy, come out and dance! It's raining!" See the difference? I was telling her to come in because it was raining and she was telling me to come out and dance because it was raining. I had a choice to make – should I continue to be the dad and say, "No honey, come in from the rain. You will get cold and wet." Or should I do something random and get in the moment with my daughter and at the same time build an amazing memory? I watched her dancing and thought, "I am going to do this with her." I walked out and for a moment it was as if time stood still while I danced in the rain with my daughter. It was beautiful, bonding, and is seared in my memory. Doing something random breaks up the mundane and allows us to see life from a different perspective. It allows us to become present in a really memorable way.

We are living in an amazing period of time. We have access to incredible amounts of information with just the touch of our figure tips. We experience more in an hour than our ancestors experienced in their entire lives. It is wonderful and thrilling. But however great our advancements are, we need to strive to have balance in our lives. It is so easy to get distracted by everything that life throws at us—including technology and all that goes with it. We have to work hard at learning to become present. We need to take advantage of the healing and inspiration that can come from being in the now, rather than perpetually living in the past, future or both. Remember to practice "Take 5." Peace and healing are found when we quiet our minds. Try it. It can be tough to do with as busy a world as ours is, but it is worth doing. Don't delay practicing the techniques listed in this chapter. Do all you can to embrace the present, be in the moment, and enjoy the now.

CHAPTER 6

Read Daily

The fourth element of my "Take 5" is reading. Reading is a crucial part of feeding your mind with positivity. If you are not pleased with your current thinking and your limiting beliefs, it is absolutely crucial that you reprogram your mind in order to have the life and world you want for yourself and your family. There are many amazing authors and leaders who can help us do this through the words that they have written. Take time for a daily session where you feed yourself with positive material – put positive in so positive can flow out (PIPO).

This may be tough at first, especially if you feel you don't have the time. We are often so busy that adding one more thing seems hard to do. If this is your situation then I recommend you start with just one minute. You can do that, right? On the other hand, if your time constraints are not too tight, I recommend you feed your mind with positive material for as much time as you can. This can be in the form of a written book, an audio file or a video. This doesn't mean reading or listening to the latest novel you've heard about. This means focusing on authors who will feed your "why" in life; authors who will remind you of your potential and greatness; authors who are seeking to enlighten you and not pull you down in your thinking; authors who will build your faith.

As you think about how much time you can devote to "positive in" everyday, consider this: We all have 24 hours in a day and we each choose how to spend every minute of those hours. Oprah Winfrey, one of the most successful people in the world today, reads and learns from so many great authors. It is one of her secrets to success in life. Is it any wonder that Warren Buffet, one of the wealthiest men on the planet, is a strong reader and is always learning more about his expertise in investing? It is said that leaders are readers. Why would this be? Leaders need to feed their why. They need to draw power, inspiration, motivation and ideas from those who have been through it. Why would you and I be any different? Just start with one minute at a time, or even better, one page at a time. I recommend you start with a book like As a Man Thinketh by James Allen. Read one page a day to begin—in the morning if you can manage it. Your mind will be filled with powerful words to start your day.

During the day you can continue to read, especially if you listen! Have you ever listened to an audiobook while working out? I listen to 1-2 books a week this way. I also listen to them in the car on the way to work, or when I'm in an airport. I do mix music into my workouts as well, but it will amaze you how much time you have to listen to a book.

What follows is a list of some of my favorite authors and books. This list is not exhaustive by any means. It is simply a snapshot of some of the books and audios that have helped me along my journey. I share the list with you in the hope that they can be of service to you during your journey. These are some of my favorites and I recommend them regularly. I hope you will take time to read them.

Books:

As a Man (or Woman) Thinketh – James Allen (I read it regularly. It's that good.)

Think and Grow Rich – Napoleon Hill

The Greatest Salesman in the World – Og Mandino

The Alchemist – Paulo Coelho

The Strangest Secret – Earl Nightingale (I recommend the audio, although you can get the written version as well. Love, love, love it. Should be standard issue in my opinion.)

Left to Tell: Discovering God Amidst the Rwandan Holocaust – Immaculee Ilibagiza (Do you want to learn about love, forgiveness and healing? This is the book for you. I have had the honor and blessing of meeting this woman and she is meant to share her message and inspire the world.)

Authors:

Deepak Chopra – I recommend anything by this man. I find him to be enlightened and healing. You can start with The Seven Spiritual Laws of Success. I have enjoyed every book that I have read so far.

Dr Joe Dispenza – I recommend his book, Breaking the Habit of being Yourself. Very transformational.

Oprah Winfrey – This woman is amazing. I love to watch her Super Soul Sundays on YouTube, listen to the meditations that she and Deepak Chopra have teamed up to do, and I read basically any book she recommends. She is an enlightened soul brought to this world to help shift the consciousness of human kind and redefine what is possible for all people. She has been quoted saying, "Books were my path to personal freedom." A great book to read by Oprah is What I Know For Sure. Powerful content from a powerful thought leader.

Dr. Wayne Dyer – I recommend any book by Dr. Dyer. He is a very enlightened author who used his life journey to help share keys to a successful, peaceful and fulfilled life. You could start with Your Erroneous Zones.

Lisa Nichols – Lisa is a person who is born to inspire. Her books are remarkable. Her seminars are transformational. And if I can say on a personal level she is a wonderful human being. Connect with her material and you wont be disappointed.

Bob Proctor – I had the honor of taking a course of his as a teenager, thanks to my parents. Hs teachings have stuck with me and inspired me throughout my life. He has many books, audios and podcasts. Choose one and start reading/listening.

Malcolm Gladwell – I recommend all his books. David and Goliath: Underdogs, Misfits, and the Art of Battling Giants is a good one to start with. It will help you feel empowered to deal with whatever challenges life has thrown your way. We all have challenges and this book helps us realize how we can turn challenges into strengths.

Gregg Braden – I recommend many of his books. The Divine Matrix is a good start. The man is brilliant.

Eckhart Tolle – He has written some very strong and empowering books. He helps unlock the understanding of how important it is to embrace the now. Start with The Power of Now.

Tony Robbins – This man brings greatness out in those he comes in contact with through his books, audios, videos and seminars.

Dr. Joe Vitale – I enjoy his style of writing. Much can be learned from his books on the law of attraction. I enjoy his teachings on the ancient Hawaiian clearing technique called, "Ho'Oponopono." Powerful inner change practice.

Robin Sharma – I love his writing style. His book, "The Monk who Sold his Ferrari" is such a powerful piece of literature.

As you start putting together a list of books you'd like to read, here are a few points to consider on the importance of reading.

What You Think, You Become

When you start a daily ritual of reading, of putting positive into your mind, you will discover that your mind is a very precious part of you and that it will take you in the direction that you guide it. I think we innately know this but we need to be constantly reminded of it. Reading from the greats help us remember. You will find less and less a desire to put negative or poor data into your mind. Over time you will be more and more cautious with what you allow into your mind. Why? Because you will learn that your mind is very impressionable and you are affected by what you feed into it, for good or for bad. You are a guardian to your mind much like you are a guardian to the food you allow to enter to your body.

You Are Meant For Greatness

The positive material you devote time to each day will remind you that you are a divine creation and that you are meant for greatness.

There Is Always A Way

You will be reminded through the experiences and wisdom of great authors that no person is meant to experience life without challenges. The fact is that each challenge can help us become more of what we are to become in life, if we let it. It is the lonely and challenging moments that define who we are and who we are becoming. You will be reminded that there is always a way in life, always. Life can be challenging but there is always a solution, so never give up.

Peace

When you give your mind daily positive input from great authors, you will learn that amidst all life can throw your way, peace can be found. Peace will come as your inner guidance system is strengthened and empowered by the positive input it receives. This will help bring you peace and help you find solutions to whatever you may experience.

Love and Gratitude

As you continue to read each day, you will find a deeper love, gratitude and appreciation for yourself, and for those around you. Love will begin to be a driving force in your life. You will find love is in you and in all creations. You will find yourself with more gratitude for what you have, which will lead to growing your faith and beliefs, which will in turn drive you towards accomplishing your dreams and goals.

Abundance

You will discover more and more as you expand your consciousness through great authors and subjects that this is a world of great abundance. We tend to think that there is not enough to go around, that if one person has something it is not as readily available for the next. This is a false and limiting belief. This world is abundant and ready for us all to tap into what we are seeking. "Ask and ye shall receive, knock and it shall be opened unto you." – Jesus Christ

Dreams

You will strive to accomplish your dreams by applying the principles and teachings you learn in your daily reading. You will do this by learning the path that others took while accomplishing their dreams. What led Thomas Edison to approach J.P. Morgan to bring the miracle of the light bulb to the world? What was the driving force behind Walt Disney creating a world of imagination and beauty in the form of animation, stories and theme parks? How about Steve Jobs and what we take for granted every day in the form of everything Apple? How about his role in Pixar and computer animation? By learning about others' dreams and what they experienced along their path, you will find courage to press on with your dreams and be inspired with new thoughts and ideas.

A Different Outlook

As you read more, you will begin to see life with a new set of eyes. Have you seen the movie Tomorrowland? It is a Disney film that examines the idea that we choose our reality. In the story, a young lady has been given a pin that, when she touches it, allows her to see life differently. At one point she touches the pin, and then asks her father, who is sitting next to her, "Did you see that?" He doesn't know what she is referring to. He cannot see what she sees. You will find that over time, as you feed your mind with positive and correct information, you will see life in a way that others often cannot see. Great authors will help you see the beauty that exists in the world and be grateful for what surrounds you. Solutions will start to present themselves in your life for all the roles you play. By expanding our knowledge, we can be inspired to leave behind our limiting beliefs and start seeing a different world.

In her book Return to Love, Marianne Williamson wrote, "Our deepest fear is not that we are inadequate, our deepest fear is that we are powerful beyond measure. It is our light not our darkness that frightens us most. We ask our ourselves, who am I to be brilliant, gorgeous, talented, fabulous?" You can insert here, "Who am I to be a good mother, father, husband, wife, lover, friend, manager, supervisor, store clerk, business owner, runner, reader? Who am I to live my dreams and become all that I can become?" And here is the most important part of the quote that I feel should be emphasized, "Actually, who are you not to be? You are a child of God and your playing small does not serve this world. We were born to make manifest the glory of God that is within us. It's not just in some of us, it's in everyone." Imagine starting your day with text such as this! You will read a text like this and see yourself differently. Who are you not to be great?

With more positive in, you will find yourself being calm and happy. You will gossip less. You will see that each person is on a journey in life and recognize that they are doing their best according to their experiences and circumstances. As your view changes, naturally you will be slower to judge others for the decisions they make.

Brain workout

As you read more, you will be giving your brain a mental workout. Just like your body needs to stay active to avoid atrophy of muscles, your brain needs to be active to avoid "thinking atrophy." You will realize there is much to be learned in our great world. As you continue and expand with your reading, you will increase your understanding of history and recognize that so much can be learned from the past mistakes and successes of the greats in this world. You will realize that you can never stop learning.

Imagine starting your day with words such as these by James Allen: "Every thought-seed sown or allowed to fall into the mind, and to take root there, produces its own, blossoming sooner or later into act, and bearing its own fruitage of opportunity and circumstances. Good thoughts bear good fruit, bad thoughts bad fruit. The outer world of circumstances shapes itself to the inner world of thought, and both pleasant and unpleasant external conditions are factors, which make for the ultimate good of the individual." Imagine putting these words into your mind to start your day. You will go into your day reminded that you are in control of what goes in, which directly impacts what comes out. You will think more before allowing a negative thought to be planted.

One of the objectives of "Take 5" is to help shift our daily habits to correct our emotions and thoughts when needed. Reading is a huge part of that. The world needs you strong—starting with you, your family, your friends, your co-workers, your neighbors, your community and everyone you come in contact with. Start each day with the best possible input so your output can be worthy of you as a divine creation.

CHAPTER 7

Dream

Previous chapters in this book discussed preparing ourselves properly by having the right mindset, being grateful, feeling love, being present and filling our minds with positive material daily. Now we are ready to move forward with the last element of "Take 5": Dreams.

Dream building and dream achieving is where many people tend to stall, fizzle out and give up. They may get excited for a bit, but when challenges arise, they lose sight of their dreams and goals and give up. So follow the previous steps and principles in this process. Don't skip any of them. Incorporating all of the principles into your daily behavior will not only help you achieve success today, but will lay the foundation for a lifetime of success and dreams come true.

Dreams do come true. As human beings, we need to dream. When we stop dreaming, it is the beginning of the end. We depend on our dreams to move us forward in life. If we are not moving forward then we are either stagnating or, worse, going backwards.

The Importance of Dreams

The dreamers of the world are so important. We depend on each other's dreams to ensure products come to market and to ensure businesses are created. We depend on dreamers to think outside the box so we can have jobs after we finish our schooling. Our dreams lead our children to the schools they would like to attend. Our dreams help us achieve the weight and look we desire. Our dreams help us get up and move to the area of the world where we have always wanted to live. Our dreams help us drive that special car or live in the home and/or neighborhood we want. Our dreams help us conquer sickness and disease. Our dreams guide us to the special person we want to spend our lives with. Our dreams bring us out of depression. Our dreams lead us to take the vacation of a lifetime. Our dreams guide us to climb that mountain, run that marathon, hike that trail, fix up that house, play that instrument, or paint that painting that we've always wanted to. Simply put, dreams help us become who we are meant to become.

What is it that you dream of? Each day I invite you to dust off your dreams and dedicate time to reviewing and evaluating your dreams. This is your time. No one is there to talk you out of it. No one is there to tell you that dreams don't come true. It is you, alone with your thoughts, emotions and beliefs, focusing your energies on what you desire out of your life. We need your dreams. We need you to pursue your dreams. We all need each other.

How to make dreams come true

Is it your dream to start a new company? To take your sales force and sales numbers to a new level? To make a certain amount of money? To lose a certain amount of weight or get into shape? Has your dream come true or is it still a challenge? What happens when dreams don't come true? Is there a formula to ensure that your dreams do come true? The answer is yes, and I have dedicated this chapter to that exact topic.

We have all experienced the letdown of dropping the ball on our dreams. It is frustrating to have a dream fall by the wayside. All too often we set a goal and start off super excited. But after we start our path, we quickly become overwhelmed and quitting becomes too easy.

I have had the opportunity to test lots of different things with regards to setting and achieving goals that range from personal athletic goals, family goals and business related goals and I have found that if I follow certain steps or guidelines my goals will and do come true.

What I have found in following my heroes in life is that whether they are conscious of it or not they will also follow these steps. I also start each day with gratitude, love, being present and reading because it is like a warm up to our dreams. They help put our mind, body and spirit in tune for dreams to happen. We don't want to give up if we are prepared to take on our dreams.

I will now highlight and discuss the 5 steps to dream-building:

STEP 1: Know where you are going

STEP 2: Have faith and believe

STEP 3: Overcome your fears

STEP 4: Break your dream up into manageable goals

STEP 5: Be patient. Don't quit.

STEP 1: Know Where You Are Going

The first step to accomplish any dream or goal is to know where you are going. It seems so simple, yet people often skip this step. State your exact goal clearly—the more clear, the better. Let's take weight loss as an example. If your dream is to lose weight, you need to be precise in your plan. How much weight do you want to lose? What size do you want your waist to be? What will your body-fat percentage be? Do you have a date set for your weight loss goals? Do you have a photo of yourself at that certain weight and size that you can look at for guidance and motivation? Is there a certain dress or suit you want to fit into? If so, what does it look like? Answering each of these questions will help you accomplish your dream because you will know where you are going.

As we figure out where we are going with our dreams, we need to be specific and we need to write things down. After writing down your goal, review it a minimum of twice daily. As Napoleon Hill teaches, this helps a person had a burning desire for their goal/dream. I grew up hearing quotes from Bob Proctor. He is one of the great leaders in setting and achieving goals. Like me, he is from the Toronto region of Ontario, Canada, and as a teenager I learned much of his goal-setting philosophy. He encouraged people to write their goals on a 3x5 card. Then he told us to carry the card with us at all times and look at it multiple times per day. I always liked this teaching–it really resonated with me.

Fast-forward several decades and I was at an event that some of our top sales people were having in Mexico. Bob Proctor was one of the keynote speakers. I was thrilled to meet one of my heroes, a man whose teachings had had such an impact on me. While backstage I introduced myself and thanked him for his influence in my life. I commented how I recalled his teachings of writing down goals and reviewing them daily. His assistant then looked at me and asked, "Joe, where is your 3x5 card?" I was somewhat taken back by this. My ego stepped in and I wanted to say something rude, but I bit my tongue. The fact of the matter was I did not have a card. I had long since stopped that process.

I went from being perplexed and bothered to inspired and motivated. How could I teach people about reaching their goals and dreams if I was not setting them? By the end of the day I had my card and it has not left me since. The only change has been that my dreams keep coming true so I have to keep updating the card. Some of the dreams written on my card are short-term goals, some are medium and some are long-term goals. Some stay on the card longer than others, but the important thing is I have them on me and I review them daily. I also have a more extended list that I have in my phone under my "notes" section.

The importance of being specific in our goals and writing them down is shown in a study done by Gail Matthews, PhD, of Dominican University. Her study involved 267 people who were asked to identify goals and work on them for four weeks. After that time, participants rated their progress and the degree to which they had accomplished their goals. The results show that the keys to successful goal achievement are:

1. Be clear on your goals and write them down.

2. Develop a plan on how you are going to achieve them.

3. Develop an accountability mechanism. This needs to be external to you. Sadly, we are not very good at keeping ourselves accountable, which is why the various weight-watching companies that require you to turn up weekly are all so successful.

Along with Bob Proctor and Gail Matthews, I encourage you to write down today what you want to accomplish in your life. This list should not be pages and pages long. Select a few specific things that you have been putting off and write them down. Be specific. If it is a car for example, I encourage you to write down the color, make, model, and year. Does it have leather or not? Does it have a good sound system? Is it coup, convertible, sedan, hatchback or truck? If it is a truck, does it have a lift? Does it have a tow package? Be specific. Then write down a date when this dream will happen. I encourage you to be realistic. Saying tomorrow may not be wise. (Not to say it couldn't happen.) Only you and possibly a significant other will know the answer to this.

I invite you to take it one step further and go to the dealership where you will purchase the vehicle, or at least to a dealership that carries the vehicle you want. Ask to sit in the vehicle. Smell the leather. Feel the steering wheel. Touch the dash and listen to the sound system. This helps to engage your senses and lock in how serious you are about this dream of yours.

STEP 2: Have faith and believe

When most people think of faith and belief they think of God and religion. This would be correct for part of the definition of faith and belief. However, I want to focus on other definitions and discussions on faith and belief. Faith is defined in the dictionary as:

1. Complete trust or confidence in someone or something.

2. Strong belief in God or in the doctrines of a religion, based on spiritual apprehension rather than proof.

What I want to focus on is your faith in you—your dreams, your talents and your abilities—and how to begin the process of transforming limiting beliefs into unlimited beliefs.

Limiting Beliefs

"One cannot be prepared for something if they secretly believe it will not happen."
– Nelson Mandela

I love music. One of my favorite bands is the Irish group U2. U2 was my first concert when I was 14 years old. My friend's older sister took a group of us to the Unforgettable Fire concert in Toronto, Canada. It was amazing. The song "Bad" was released on that album and it is one of my favorite songs. It is a powerful song about drug addiction. When hearing this song over the years, I would reflect on how sad drug addiction must be for people. It has always been a song to make me reflect. However, I was recently listening to it, as I frequently do, and for some reason the lyrics meant something different to me at this moment in time. I realized that although we may not be addicted to drugs or alcohol or some other physically addictive vice, how many of us walk around day in and day out addicted to "limiting beliefs"? Addicted to negative self speak and self-doubt? These limiting beliefs become like a crutch that we lean on and in many instances we don't even realize it.

Why are limiting beliefs holding us back? It is said that 95 percent of what we do is subconscious. That means we have stuff programmed into our brain that we may not even know exists and this also is our limiting beliefs. Wallace Wattles, who wrote The Science of Getting Rich, says, "Having read this you must believe that it is possible for you to succeed; but it is not enough for you to believe that you can. You must know that you can and the subconscious mind must know it as well as the objective mind . . . People fail because they think, objectively, that they can do things, but do not know, subconsciously, that they can do them. It is more likely that your subconscious mind is even now impressed with doubts of your ability to succeed; and these must be removed, or it will withhold its power when you need it most." This explains why you may be doing everything right, from saying the right thing, thinking positively, and writing it down, but not seeing results. Our subconscious mind is powerful and needs to be considered.

Here are a few examples of some of the limiting beliefs that are often times conditioned into our thinking:

- I will never get ahead in life.
- I will always be from this side of the tracks or this side of town.
- Success is not for me.
- Nothing good ever happens to me.
- Positive thinking doesn't work.
- I can't sell.
- If I only said…
- If I only did…
- If that person (example: a coach) only played me in that game then I would be…
- I will never forgive myself.
- I will never forgive him or her for what they did/said/didn't say/didn't do.
- I'm too short.
- I'm too tall.
- I'm clumsy.
- My body is not beautiful enough.
- I look horrible in pictures.
- I am dumb. I am a bad student. I am not a reader.
- Dating that girl or guy is out of my league.
- Stop being a dreamer.
- Happiness is a myth.
- People with money are crooks.
- Statements like, "Must be nice," or "In a million years."
- I could never in my wildest dreams believe I could have a vacation like that person. Or drive a car like that. Or live in a home like that.
- Dreams coming true is a myth.

- Our family attracts bad luck.
- Good fortune has never been my thing.
- Being fat runs in my family. There is no hope for me.
- My dad had a short fuse; therefore, I am not patient.
- I am ugly.
- I'm a loser.
- I'm an idiot.
- I'm not athletic.

Do any of these sound familiar? If you find yourself speaking any of these words and possibly playing them over and over in your mind, then you may have an addiction to limiting beliefs. Sure, it is not a physical addiction, so how bad can it be? The truth is that beliefs like these can hold you back from moving in the direction of a more positive life and the life that can and should be yours. They may very well be holding you back from being happy and feeling fulfilled. They may be holding you back from having wonderful, healthy family and friend relationships. All of this tends to cause a person to give up on dreams and jump back on the treadmill of life that doesn't seem to be going anywhere. If this is where you find yourself then you are not alone, my friend. It is more common than you think.

The U2 song "Bad" says, "If I could, yes I would; If I could, I would let it go." There may be different interpretations to these lyrics but to me, I hear that in order for us to begin moving forward and shedding limiting beliefs, we must first have a desire to "let it go." We have to let go of what is holding us back from moving forward and becoming all we are on this earth to become.

I will share a personal example of this and I want you to consider what might be lingering in your mind and soul. At an early age, reading did not come naturally to me. I came to a conclusion that I was not a reader. I started telling myself this. I said to myself and others, "I am not a reader" or "I am not a strong reader." It was always my excuse for not reading. This stuck with me throughout my life. Sure, I would read some books but they were far and few between. I recognized several years ago that this was a limiting belief and that I could turn my supposed weakness into strength. I started working on this area of my life and now I read every day and go through 2-4 books per month, as well as several audio books per month. I had a dream to read more and I had to reprogram my mind to believe I could do it. I now say daily to myself, "I am a reader," or "I am a strong reader."

How did I re-program my mind in this area of my life? The answer is that I did the "Take 5" activities that are presented in this book. As you practice these five points daily, you will find your limiting beliefs melting away and having less a hold on you. Take for instance gratitude. Gratitude leads to faith, which will draw you towards thinking higher thoughts of yourself and what you are trying to accomplish. Do this daily as often as needed. It sets a great base for growth. When we link our thoughts, dreams and desires with emotion, we attract powerfully that which we are seeking. This is why gratitude and love are so crucial to creating lasting change.

I express gratitude for having eyes to see and a brain to process what I am seeing and reading. I am grateful for authors who have taken the time to write amazing books that help me become all I can become. I am grateful for the gift of sight. Helen Keller said, "I have often thought it would be a blessing if each human being were stricken blind and deaf for a few days during his early adult life. Darkness would make him more appreciative of sight; silence would teach him the joys of sounds." These are powerful words from someone who knows something about living in darkness and silence.

I had an experience while doing Ironman St. George several years ago. One thing I like about Ironman and endurance sports is that it is like putting life into an event. You have highs, lows, exciting times and lonely moments that are dark. You have to manage what you eat and control your thoughts. You need to have faith, create a plan, encourage people, take encouragement, be patient and in many cases endure and not give up. At the time I did it, the St. George Ironman was considered by some to be the toughest Ironman in the world. I can see why. It beat me up. I had a decent swim and bike, but then came the run.

After about three miles of running there was a steep hill and it was brutal. My stomach was completely off due to my nutrition during the swim and bike. I did not do a good job managing my electrolytes and ended up unable to properly process liquids or any food. By this point the temperatures were hovering around 93 degrees and the wind was starting to pick up. I had a blister that seemed to cover the entire bottom of my foot. I witnessed a few people collapse from the heat, and all I could do was to walk. Needless to say, I was done physically and emotionally. I turned very negative on the elements and also on myself. I was embarrassed because my parents were there to see me, my mother-in-law was there, my kids were there and friends were watching. I was in a state of shame, and that is not a good place to be. I started on a string of negative and destructive thoughts that were bringing me down further by the minute. This went on for hours during the run (which I was walking).

Then something magical happened. I was somewhere around mile 22 or 23, and I was quite delirious. It was getting dark and I was coming down a crazy hill. I was watching a lady approach me, and I couldn't figure out what was different about her. As she got closer I realized she had a prosthetic leg. I was overcome. As she passed, I told her how much she inspired me and encouraged her as she was going up the hill. Suddenly I had emotions of gratitude flooding through every cell of my body. I realized that if she could overcome challenges that were greater than my own, then I could do the same. I started to run again and with a strategy of run/walk, I finished that event.

What was different? I still had a blister. I was still drained by the heat of the sun. There was still wind. My stomach was still all messed up. What was different was my gratitude helped changed my perspective. Suddenly, I was no longer focused on my challenges but on my blessings. My gratitude gave me hope. My challenges were suddenly something I needed to overcome rather than something that caused me to want to complain and possibly give up. I stopped the destructive self-talk and I looked for solutions and was able to draw motivation. I was able to then encourage others.

Again, it's important to understand that as we feed our conscious mind with daily positive material, we begin the process of changing the limiting beliefs that have been programmed into our subconscious mind. If we do this, we can change our direction in life. We become that which dominates our thoughts because we are changing the programming of what we believe is possible in life.

I am

I would now like to introduce you to the idea of acting as if something you dream of is already reality. In his book The Divine Matrix, Gregg Braden quotes Neville Goddard: "Neville states so clearly in his description of faith, through the act of persisting in the assumption that your desire is already fulfilled your world inevitably conforms to your assumption." Think about this for a moment. You may never have considered faith in this manner. Think back to the quotes I shared earlier about how we become what we think about. In Mark 11:24, Jesus said, "Therefore I say unto you, what things soever ye desire, when ye pray, believe that ye receive them, and ye shall have them." I don't like to say things like "If I only had," or "I wish I could" or "someday." I like being specific and starting a sentence with "I am."

- I am abundance
- I am happy
- I am prosperity
- I am love
- I am patient
- I am kind
- I am gratitude
- I am joy
- I am bliss
- I am Ironman (This happens to be a focus of mine, but if you are training for a 5K, 10K, half marathon or marathon, you could say that.)
- I am my perfect weight
- I am perfect health
- I am a reader
- I am attracting wealth
- I am attracting ideas

There is something empowering about saying these words. I invite you today to try this. Take happiness for example. If for whatever reason you have a hard time being happy, then say to yourself "I am happy," or "I am abundance of happiness." The Dalai Lama says, "Faith dispels doubt and hesitation, it liberates you from suffering and delivers you to the city of peace and happiness."

There are some schools of thinking that say to try and hold a positive thought for at least 20 seconds, but I recommend one minute or more. Focus on the "I am" through thought, prayer, meditation, or just by repeating it to yourself. Watch magic happen in your day. You will find yourself attracting happiness. You will find yourself not only being happier, but you will find things that are just... happy. People, situations, literature and songs that inspire you and help you be happy will all be attracted to you. Repeat this several times during the day. If you find yourself slipping during the day, which is normal, then repeat the mantra of "I am abundance of happiness," or "I am happy" and hold it for a certain period of time. Maybe have a copy of the book with you and read even one paragraph. You have the power within you to literally snap out of a negative mood and into a place of peace and happiness. Use "I am" in whatever way you want (prayer, meditation, yoga, quiet time, etc.). I do this very thing. I know it works.

As we have discussed, about 95% of what we do is subconscious. It is said by some that much of our belief system is programmed by as early as the age of 6 and fully "locked in" by our mid-30s. This part of "Take 5" is key and a little more advanced.

Through the practice of meditation, we are able to quiet our conscious mind in such a way to access our subconscious mind and to begin the process of reprogramming it. Our beliefs have been learned; therefore, they can be "unlearned." You may need professional help to do this, so please seek whatever help you may need. However, I believe that for most of us, we are able to do this. This book is not to teach meditation, so I encourage you to dig deeper on this subject (there are hundreds of books and websites that provide everything you'll need to develop effective meditation techniques). However, I would like to share what has worked for me:

1. I first work on quieting my mind. For some it can be done without music. For me, I find meditation music is very helpful. I use what are called "induction" techniques to quiet my mind. I have my own technique that is a variation of going through my entire body, focusing on each part from head to toe. My variation is this: I list each organ and body system, expressing gratitude and love for each.

2. I focus on one or maybe two of my limiting beliefs. I also start using faith to change that belief to a positive one by saying, "I am _____." For instance, I may say, "I am a strong reader" or "I am abundance" or "I am love," and so forth. I commit 30-60 minutes for this sort of meditation. I shoot for making this a daily behavior, and it is incredible the difference it has made in my life.

3. I visualize my life free of these limiting beliefs. I also visualize the changes I want to make in my life. When we learn something, including a belief about ourselves, it is being filed into our subconscious mind and neural connections are being made. The more we reinforce these beliefs by feeding them and reminding ourselves of them, the more the connection solidifies. To help me "unlearn" these limiting beliefs and fears, I imagine and visualize these connections coming apart. It is my own simple approach to it. I

visualize them being disconnected much like cutting a cord, rope or wire. For some it can happen very quickly. But for most of us it takes time. Be patient with yourself. Be patient with the process. My example of "I am not a reader" had been with me my whole life from the time I learned how to read. That's a long time. Consider a limiting belief that you have and how long it has been connected to you. How often do you feed it? Interesting question. In some cases you may also have been feeding it and reinforcing it for your whole life. Be patient and be consistent.

Forgive and forget

Sometimes we focus too much on mistakes we made in the past, or worry about mistakes that might happen in the future. Either way, we allow limiting beliefs to fester like an old wound that will never heal. The past—which includes our past mistakes and failures, and others' past mistakes and failures—is already past. Those mistakes and failures don't exist anymore unless we allow them to continue in our minds. All we have is the present. So why throw away the present worrying about the past and not forgiving yourself or others? We can replay scenarios and conversations in our minds of things that have already passed, all the while missing the miracle of the present. Forgiveness is healing and must happen in our lives to allow us to become all that we can become. Forgiveness is part of shedding our limiting beliefs. Don't hold on anymore. It is the past. Work on forgiving yourself and then move to forgiving others. Don't hold on another day.

I love the words in "Redemption Song," Bob Marley which says, "Emancipate yourselves from mental slavery, none but ourselves can free our minds." It starts with you. You are important. The world needs you. Make a decision today to set your mind free and start on your road to light and personal growth.

STEP 3: Overcome your fears

"Life begins where fear ends." – Osho

Fear kills dreams. Fear actually keeps people from even leaving the starting blocks. Consider the dream of losing weight and having that certain body: "What if I start the process, and then I don't succeed? I may as well just stay at this weight and not even try." There is a reason so many people talk about "overcoming fear" as part of success in life. Fear cripples us. It holds us back from achieving our potential in life.

The interesting thing about fear is it is learned. Some say there are natural fears that we are born with, such as a fear of heights or a fear of death. This could be the case, but I want to focus on the fears that hold us back in life, the fears that are learned. I believe that the majority of fears are learned.

Fear is learned and can therefore be unlearned. There is a saying my father used to quote to us quite regularly while growing up. FEAR stands for: False, Evidence, Appearing, Real. This simple statement can help us look at this four-letter word differently. Here are few common fears that I believe are learned during our journey through this mortal experience:

- Fear of failure
- Fear of success
- Fear of what people will think of us
- Fear of risk
- Fear of poverty
- Fear of rejection
- Fear of people (friends, family, different races or nationalities)
- Fear of speaking in front of a crowd
- Fear of the telephone
- Fear of money
- Fear of change
- Fear of commitment
- Fear of being alone
- Fear of leadership
- Fear of being in control of your own destiny
- Fear of getting out of your comfort zone
- Fear of the unknown
- Fear of food
- Fear of the opposite sex
- Fear of asking for the sale
- Fear of getting sick and disease
- Fear of becoming over weight

Any of these sound familiar? You are not alone. We all have fears that we have picked up during our lives. No one is immune to fears. However, what separates those who go on to do great things and accomplish their dreams is that they overcome their fears; not once, not twice, but continuing the process throughout their lives as they find success in their different projects.

I want to discuss the first fear on the list—the fear of failure—and then I will share five points that help me overcome fears in life.

Replace Your Thoughts of Fear

When a thought of fear enters your mind, chase it away with a positive thought of love. Love and fear cannot exist simultaneously. Another way to replace your fearful thoughts is immediately think of your dreams and goals. Chase them out. "Fear be gone!" This is one reason to carry your written dreams with you. Another system of chasing out fears is to turn your smart phone into a library of written books, as well as audio books. If you're standing in line at the store and fears start to kick in, turn on that book or start reading it. How about while driving in the car and the fears start to creep up? Stop the car, find that audio book you have on CD or on your phone and listen to it. Chase those fears away.

Fear of failure

"Fear of failure is what keeps most people from achieving their dreams."
– The Alchemist by Paulo Coelho

As I have mentioned, I am a father of 4 children: 3 boys and 1 daughter. Each child has passions. I travel a lot so I take them on a trip a year that is focused on them and possibly something they are passionate about and would like to do. For example, my older son loves to be in the mountains hiking and camping. I have started climbing the 7 summits with him and have already accomplished Kilimanjaro in Africa and Elbrus in Russia. Our second son is an avid skier, hiker, climber, camper and overall outdoor enthusiast. He will select something adventurous each time.

Our third son currently loves to ski and play his kendama, and also recently went through a phase of skateboarding. A few years ago, to support his skateboarding passion, we took a father and son trip to a skateboarding fundraiser in California to see his idol at that time—Ryan Sheckler—and other pros skate and raise money for a worthy cause.

Having not spent a lot of time around skate boarding I was not very aware of what a person goes through to become a pro and learn the crazy tricks we see them do. I also had some stereotypes in my mind of a bunch of "skate punks" who had long hair, tattoos and attitudes to go with it.

We arrived at the event and guess what? There was some long hair and some tattoos. But was I in for a learning experience in overcoming the fear of failure. We watched these professional skateboarders try a trick and come up short. They tried the trick again and came up short. Again and again they tried but repeatedly failed. I am talking for hours.

The average observer would see this as failure. But when they finally got it, wow, it was amazing. I was so very impressed with their persistence in not giving up. I was also impressed that even though they had hundreds of spectators watching them, they were not afraid to work on their moves and be viewed as failing before they landed their trick. When they fell, we are not talking about falling onto grass or into a foam pit. They were falling onto concrete. So their fear of failing must be at moments very intense. But when they landed their trick, the cameras were ready and what a spectacular experience.

Again, I was amazed and my admiration for these athletes went up 50 notches that day. May I add I also was impressed with their desires to raise money for a worthy cause and help children in need. Well done, Ryan Sheckler and team.

Fear of failure holds us back. The fear of failure is a standard fear, but one that must be overcome. Imagine how many ideas might have dust collecting on them because a person is afraid of moving forward because they don't want to fail. We are taught at an early age to not fail. We are taught to avoid failure, taught to avoid risk. Isn't that interesting? Interesting because in our society we rely on risk takers to create new companies, new ideas, new brands. Such creation leads to new jobs and helps the economy to function. Think about it: the entire schooling system is feeding people through so they can get jobs and have employment. But who is creating the jobs? It is the dreamers of the world who are stepping out of the box and taking risks who are creating the jobs. We rely on people who see failure as a stepping-stone toward a worthy creation.

Consider the following thoughts and points that keep us from reaching out for our dreams:

"Don't fail with your homework. You need to pass."

"Don't fail with that winning shot and let down the team."

"Don't fail the test/exam."

"Don't get below a certain grade for your ACT or you will not get into 'that' school."

"Don't fail in that project at work."

"Play it safe."

"The art project is X and needs to be done the way it is requested. Stay within the boundaries."

"8 out of 10 start-up companies fail." (I have heard all sorts of stats but this is one that we hear most regularly.)

"I don't want to try out for that team or enter that event because I don't want to fail."

We often hear words like, "Don't fail me." This is unfortunate, because if we were taught to not fear failure, we would recognize that it is through failure that we grow and develop and perfect the very thing that will and can bring us to success in life. This is the process of learning what works and what doesn't work. A child would never learn how to walk if they were afraid of failure. Consider the early years of a child's life, which happens to be one of the greatest growing periods for a human. Young children fail over and over and over, but they keep trying and learning. Much can be learned from watching a child.

Earl Nightingale defines success as "the progressive realization of a worthy ideal." Progressive realization implies that it is ongoing. If that is true then failure truly is part of the journey that leads us to great outcomes. Don't let fear of failure paralyze your thoughts and dreams. When I think about things I have not done, it is often because I was afraid to fail. What if I don't finish this and look like a fool? What if I try this or that and people laugh at me? Why even try if I could fail? Dr. Wayne Dyer teaches that failure really doesn't exist. Think about it. Why should we accept someone's judgment of whether we failed or not? Consider this quote by one of the greatest of greats, Michael Jordan. "I've missed more than 9000 shots in my career. I've lost almost 300 games. 26 times, I've been trusted to take the game winning shot and missed. I've failed over and over and over again in my life. That is why I succeed." People who are successful think of failures as stepping-stones on their road to success.

So what can be done? Here is my personal approach to overcoming my fears. Please note that each of these fall under a simple statement by Max Lucado: "Feed your fears and your faith will starve. Feed your faith, and your fears will." If you feed your fears, expect your fears to remain alive and well and hold you back from becoming all you can become. However, if you starve your fears and feed your dreams, conquering your fears is inevitable. The following steps help me support my dreams and maximize my chances of overcoming my fears. They will do the same for you, allowing you to get on to the life you dream of, the life you deserve.

1) Love

2) Recognize that fear is learned and can therefore be unlearned

3) Don't feed your fears—feed your whys and dreams

4) Do that which you fear to overcome fear

5) Surround yourself with people who will help you overcome fear

Love

"Fear knocked on the door. Love answered and no one was there."
-Unknown

As I discussed earlier in the book, I have a desire to improve my golf game. One thing that is difficult for me when it comes to golf is a fear of failure and embarrassment. Along my journey, I had a particularly bad golf game with a friend of mine. He is an amazing golfer and very patient with me, but my ego got in the way and I was embarrassed because I thought I was failing. My fear was becoming my reality. It was as if I was playing for the first time and was using a baseball bat rather than a golf club. If you play golf you understand that this is very discouraging. I was ready to throw in the towel.

Then I remembered something I had read by Deepak Chopra about the power of love in our lives. I was inspired to look at my fear of failure in golf with a spirit of love. The next night, I went back to the golf course and picked up my clubs again. This time, I approached the game in a spirit of love. Magically, I was in control; calm, cool and collected while I played with love and hope. I have a long way to go with my golf game and I am committed to looking at it through love rather than fearing to fail.

Do you think for a moment that Michael Jordan feared failure? I am sure it concerned him, but he overcame it time and time again. Fear can be conquered, starting with love. Love starts with the basic foundation of loving yourself. Self-love will help you love those around you. Develop a love for whatever you are afraid to fail at, and watch how this love and passion will help you find a way. I believe love is the base of overcoming fear. Choose love over fear and watch the words of Virgil ring true—"love conquers all."

Fear Is Learned and Can Therefore Be Unlearned

Whatever fears you have were learned. How do we learn these fears? We learn fears in so many ways: school, experiences, family, friends, TV, media, movies, magazines and articles. Just watching another person being afraid can make us suddenly fear something. I believe the first thing we can do to unlearn a fear is to control the media content that we watch. The media has the ability to create fear in the population with their stories. Let's take for example the fear of sharks. This is one that surfaces regularly due to an unfortunate shark encounter. Suddenly the public is freaked out and afraid of sharks and, in some cases, the water. You may have experienced it personally or watched another person suddenly afraid of the water. These stories cause us to become fixated in fear. Yet, according to the Florida Museum of Natural History, "The international Shark Attack File investigated 130 incidents of alleged shark-human interaction occurring worldwide in 2014. Upon review, 72 of these incidents represented confirmed cases of unprovoked shark attacks on humans." The rest were provoked or brought on by swimming in a tank or grabbing a shark or trying to feed one. So, I would say that 72 out of the tens of millions of people who swim and play in the ocean every year is a pretty safe statistic to go by. And although we don't want to ever see a person die from an encounter with a shark, the number is less than 20 per year worldwide. This doesn't mean there is no chance, but to put this on the news and get people fearing sharks is not right. This is not to say

I am disrespecting any readers who may have had an encounter with a shark. I am just pointing out the reality of this and how the news uses fear to sell.

A theme that I keep coming back to is we become what we think about. Another way to describe this is that we attract what dominates our minds. This includes our fears. Isn't it interesting that sharks can sense fear? It is called electroperception. They detect very slight electrical pulses in the water. So, if we are creating fear in the population, in this particular case to do with sharks, then people go into the water in masses around the world with this fear and it is in essence attracting exactly that which they fear.

Consider the number of fearful studies that are regularly highlighted in the media on health and disease, automobile and place accidents, the foods we eat, the economy and unemployment rates, wars, hate crimes, divorce statistics, and the list goes on. All this kind of news just works to feed our fears. I am not saying there is no good in the media. Of course there is some good. What I am saying is be cautious what you are allowing into your mind and your life. We become what we think about and if we are constantly being reminded of the negatives to do with our health and wellness, the economy and hate crimes, it is my belief that we attract this into our lives.

Let's take fear of failure as an example, because it is so common. We have been conditioned to believe that failure is wrong and should be avoided at all cost. No one wants to be a failure. Or do we? I believe the first thing that needs to happen is we need to change our perception of failure. Instead of thinking of failure as something we need to avoid, we should look at failure as part of our road to success. No great company, no great brand, no great athlete, no great idea, no great dream has existed without working through failures along the way. Once we can change our perception of failure, we can start unlearning our fear of failure. One of the best ways to do this is to read every day from great books that exist in the world. Read about how brands were born. Read about great inventors. Read about great athletes and learn about their journey to success. Follow the people you admire in business, sports, music and movies on social media and pick up pointers about what got them to where they are. You will find that they talk about overcoming fears in order to get where they are.

Please be aware that there is a difference between fear and danger. Fear is learned, but danger is real and needs to be respected. They tend to go hand and hand, but I believe they are different. I like what Will Smith's character had to say about fear in the movie After Earth: "Fear is not real. The only place that fear can exist is in our thoughts of the future. It is a product of our imagination, causing us to fear things that do not at present and may not ever exist. That is near insanity. Do not misunderstand me; danger is very real, but fear is a choice." The fears we can choose to unlearn are the fears in our personal lives that we must conquer in order to move forward with our dreams.

Don't Feed Your Fears—Feed Your Whys And Dreams

We become whatever dominates our thoughts. If we fear something and dwell on it, we activate the law of attraction to our fears rather than our dreams. But it can work both ways—if we dwell on things we want to accomplish, we will activate the law of attraction to our dreams. Allow me to share a personal experience to explain this thought. I love to trail run. Trail running is different than running on pavement because a trail has rocks and roots and is a generally uneven surface. I used to have the habit of tripping quite regularly. I was like a magnet to every rock and root that existed along a trail. It is normal to trip from time to time, but not consistently like I was doing. It started to become a fear of mine and I focused on it quite a lot.

Recently, I was out running and listening to an audio that was discussing the law of attraction. Suddenly I realized that I had been running for close to five miles and had not tripped once. The thought occurred to me that I was attracting fear while running because my fear of tripping would dominate my thoughts each time I went out. Sure enough, as my thoughts turned to my fear, I tripped three times in less than two minutes. It was nuts. I stopped mid-trail to take a breather and literally shake it off. I cleared my mind and changed what was going through my thoughts. Rather than focus on what I feared, which was tripping and falling, I thought of myself as light as a feather, floating effortlessly over the trail. I went the remainder of my run, another five miles or so, without a single problem.

Since that day I have tripped a few times while running, but it only happens when I let my mind wander to my fears of falling. Getting over this fear is a work in progress and I am working to conquer it. James Allen said, "The soul attracts that which it secretly harbors; that which it loves and also that which it fears." Note how he says, "secretly harbors." I believe that our subconscious mind can have deep fears that have been learned throughout our lives. For this reason we must fill our minds and hearts with our dreams and "whys" in life, rather than feeding our fears. This is a very important point in overcoming fears. Choose wisely the books you read, the shows you watch, the material that is programming your mind and your very being. Everything you put into your mind affects who you are becoming in life. So what will it be? Will you attract the roots and rocks in your life, or will you attract your dreams of running smoothly? It truly is your choice.

"Every thought-seed sown or allowed to fall into the mind, and to take root there, produces its own, blossoming sooner or later into act, and bearing its own fruitage of opportunity and circumstance. Good thoughts bear good fruit, bad thoughts bad fruit."
– James Allen

Do That Which You Fear to Overcome Fear

Mark Twain once brilliantly said, "Do the thing you fear the most and the death of fear is certain." I have lived by this a lot in my life. Act on what you fear and you will find that it is not that scary after all. As a teenager I had an experience that taught me this lesson. It was my 9th grade year (grade 9 for my friends in Canada), and like most 9th graders, I was worried about what others thought. I wanted to make a good impression. I lived in a small town in Ontario, Canada, and I was a bit different from other kids in many ways—one way in particular was that I was a breakdancer. It was a passion of mine. However, I kept it mostly to myself, particularly around the high school. I was worried what people might think. There were a few kids in my school who did not like me to begin with, and I did not want to fuel that in any way. In a nutshell, I feared what might happen if I came out in public as a breakdancer in my school. It was a small school so some people knew, but I was certainly not busting out my cardboard in the halls and breakdancing.

As fate would have it, there was a school talent show that year. I was encouraged to breakdance at this event. At first I was afraid. What would the school think? What would the girls think? Would I ever be able to get a date after that? What would the guys who didn't really like me think? What if I froze on stage and just couldn't dance? If I failed then I would have to go through the next three years of my life as the guy who botched it on stage in front of the school. So many fears were flowing through my mind as I struggled to make the decision. But I finally decided I would do it.

Once I had decided I would perform, I started practicing. I did the best a 9th grader could do to prepare for that moment. The time came. I was backstage and fear was pulsating through my entire being. I was freaked out. All the fears I just mentioned, as well as a few new ones, were taking over. I remember being in my little breakdancing pose, waiting for the curtains to open, and thinking something like, "It's hero or chump time." No turning back. When the curtains opened and the music started I went into my routine and guess what? When I started "doing," my fears melted away. It felt great to just do. Was it a perfect routine? No, I made mistakes. Did some people walk away laughing at me? I am sure that happened. But I walked away pleased with my performance and, for the most part, the crowd enjoyed it. All the fears that I had built in my mind were put to rest from the doing. It was a defining moment in my life. I am grateful that my fears did not hold me back.

When we take action, when we "do," there is something that happens within us that changes our fear to courage. So consider Mark Twain's advice and do something you are afraid of. Some examples may include:

If you are afraid to love, love.

If you are afraid to commit, commit.

If you are a sales person and you are afraid of the follow up, follow up.

If you are trying to get in shape and afraid to start because you don't want to fail, start and do.

If you are afraid to make a decision because you fear the unknown or the outcome, then study out your decision and move forward and act.

If you are afraid to ask that girl or guy out on a date, just ask.

If you are afraid to try to bring that idea to market, study it out, create a plan and try.

If you are afraid to pick up the phone and call someone, pick it up and call.

If you are afraid to forgive, forgive.

If you are afraid to ask forgiveness, ask forgiveness.

If you are afraid to fly, get help if needed and get out there and fly.

If you are afraid to talk to your spouse or significant other about something that needs to be discussed, just reach out and talk.

If you are afraid to talk to people, go up and talk to someone.

If you are afraid of heights, get with people who will safely help you overcome this fear and start being around heights.

It is not always easy to overcome fear and you may, in some instances, require professional help. That is okay. Don't fear experts along your path to overcoming fear. More often than not, however, just by consistently "doing" you will overcome your fears. Note how I said consistently. It is not just doing something once. Like a muscle you need to practice to get stronger over time. It is a process and you will get better at it. And one day you will look back and say, "Wow, I can't believe I was ever afraid of that."

Surround Yourself With People Who Will Help You Overcome Fear

"We become the combined average of the five people we are around the most." – Jim Rohn

I had a great experience with my oldest son where I became the student and he the teacher. He showed interest at an early age in the sport of rock climbing. I decided to learn along with him and his brothers and it has been a great journey. Recently, we were climbing a beautiful desert tower in Arches National Park. He was the lead climber and I was belaying him at the bottom. This particular climb has two pitches. The last pitch is only a few meters but it is a second pitch just the same. He reached the top of the first pitch and set up a belay system to bring me safely to that point. Although I found it challenging, I was able to reach the first pitch just fine. It was the second pitch that spooked me in a way I had never been spooked before. To the right of it was several hundred-foot drop down into a valley. Beautiful view, but was I scared. Fear took over my body from head to toe.

I knew I was safe since I was connected to my son who was belaying me to the top, and I knew it was a distance of only about 2 meters. But the thought of a drop several hundred feet down on the other side got into my head and I was afraid. I stood there, not able to move. My son said, "Dad, I have you. You can do this. It is totally safe." He reminded me of the rigging and showed me how each point connected. I was impressed with all he had learned over the years. He reminded me of the gear and how well they are rated from a safety perspective. But I was still frozen with fear. Then he said, "Dad, remember all the things you have taught me about overcoming fear. You have this." I was comforted by his words and then I uttered the phrase, "Do the thing you fear the most and the death of fear is certain." I literally shook it off and went for it. Of course I chose not to look down to my right. Instead I looked straight ahead and finished the climb by going to the top. It felt amazing.

I am grateful my son was there at a time when I could use his confidence to help me achieve my goal. Although it was an extreme situation, it represents that we can become frozen with fear in so many ways, unless we have someone who will encourage us to go for our dreams. Left on our own it is much easier to give up. We all need the boost and support from people who will help us reach our dreams and make them a reality.

I have amazing business partners who help feed my "whys" and remind me of my great potential, both in life and our businesses.

They help remind me of our goals and we support one another. For example, I speak to my business partners virtually every day, and we review our goals and dreams throughout our conversations. We will help correct each other if we appear to be off. If we are having an off day, we help one another turn our emotions around in a positive direction. Our dreams are too important to allow the opposite to happen, so be sure to surround yourself with those who will help you achieve your dreams and aspirations rather than drag you down.

Let's take for example a goal that many people make at the beginning of a new year—the goal to lose weight and/or get into shape. It is scary for many people to go into that sort of commitment. Fear of failure is high. You say to yourself, "I've tried this before and it did not work." You hear stories about how the gyms are full in January and then half way through the month of February they are back to normal. You are fearful that you will be part of the group that drops out in February. Will you have the willpower to make it? Can you adjust your eating habits in such a way to maximize your weight and/or health and wellness goals? How will you wake up each day and do what is necessary to accomplish your goals?

One way to help reach the goal is to have an accountability partner or partners. This is becoming a popular thing in gyms across the country. Some may see the word "accountability" and have thoughts of a taskmaster pop into their head. But really, what this means is you have one or more people who are working along side you towards a common goal. They will be there for you as you need them and you will be there when they need you. The chances of success are much greater when you have people to share the journey with you. Your journey becomes easier. However, select wisely who your partner(s) will be. You don't want a "negative ninny" as part of your group, unless of course you are so strong that you will help them through the moments when they want to quit.

Another way to help achieve a goal is to have a coach. Coaches are very good at helping achieve goals ranging from exercise to health and wellness, to starting a business or taking up painting. Whatever you want to do, be sure to surround yourself with people who will help you and not drag you down. As your fear of failure creeps in, let your partner(s) know. Don't be afraid to ask for encouragement. We all need each other in life and surrounding ourselves with people who we can trust and who will be there for us improves our chances of success. Our fear of failure will melt over time as our confidence grows. The support of others can help us achieve this confidence.

Remember that your fears have been built over years and years, so be patient. Be patient with yourself and the process you will be going through. In some cases, you will find that conquering fears will happen very quickly. With some of your more deep-rooted fears it may take more time. If you have very deep fears you may need professional help on your path to overcoming. Whatever your journey ahead holds for you, you can do it. There is always a way. Conquering your fears will allow you to enjoy your pathway to freedom and life success.

STEP 4: Break Your Dream Up Into Manageable Goals

It is easy to get excited about a dream but when we start applying our action plan, if we even get to that point, we can fail very quickly.

The reason why is simply that our mind sees the ultimate goal, but it is hard to accept all that needs to happen to get to that ultimate goal. The result is that we quit. To avoid this scenario, I propose that you break up your dream into short-term, medium-term and long-term goals. This will give you the chance to not feel overwhelmed and also gives you the chance to celebrate along your path. This is very important.

As I approach any goal, I break it up into bite-size goals. This applies to reading a book or doing an endurance event. I create bite-size goals that lead me towards my ultimate long-term goal. A good example is weight loss. If your dream is to lose 20 pounds and you wake up after week one and you have lost only one pound, what is your likelihood of continuing? Pretty slim. So many people drop out after seeing these results.

However, if you set some short-term goals, such as losing one or two pounds this week, then five pounds by the end of two weeks, then medium-term goals of 10 pounds, 15 pounds and so on until you reach your ultimate goal of 20 pounds, the goal is reachable because you have a plan that includes "wins" along the way.

This same process applies to all dreams you may have. Try it. It works like a charm. I also encourage you to celebrate when you reach each short, medium and long-term goal that you set.

STEP 5: Be patient. Don't quit.

We live in a world of instant gratification. We expect a pill to instantly fix whatever sickness we have. We expect that when we type a question on our computer the answer will instantly appear. If we want a car or a house or a couch or whatever it may be, there is some person or organization that will help us get it even if we are not financially ready to buy it. Why is it any different with our dreams? We may not be saying that, but that is how we perceive it. We want our dreams to happen now, but that is not how it works in life. Having patience and not quitting is crucial to the dream-building process. Have you every heard a great leader or sports hero say, "Seriously, it is just too hard chasing your dreams. Why don't you just quit? Why waste your time? Do yourself a favor and quit now. Statistics are not on your side. Quit now." Clearly no successful person has ever said words like these. Patience and not quitting are part of every successful person's journey. Every great person. No exceptions.

This doesn't mean to say that you keep doing the exact same thing and get the exact same results. What I am saying is that if your dream is strong enough and it is something you truly want to accomplish, then you remind yourself that there is always a way. If it doesn't work one way then you look for another option. If that option doesn't work then you try another route, always keeping in mind what you are ultimately trying to accomplish. Think about the brands and companies that you rely on and are passionate about in your life. Think about your sports heroes and the TV/movie personalities you admire. Each of them has a story of not quitting on their dreams. Here are a few of my favorite examples of great people who didn't give up on their dreams.

Steve Jobs

I am grateful that after being fired by the very company he started, Steve Jobs did not quit. He went on to fund and help start Pixar, and then returned to Apple to lead it to become one of the greatest brands of all time. I use an iPhone, an Apple laptop and an Apple watch. I listen to audio books on my iPhone, I listen to music on my iPhone, I read books on my iPhone, I get questions answered on my iPhone, I get directions on my iPhone, I watch shows with my kids on my iPhone, I play games on my iPhone and I make notes on my iPhone—and that's just to name a few. My goodness, am I grateful that Steve Jobs did not quit on his dreams.

Ed Catmull

Speaking of Pixar and Steve Jobs, the story of Pixar goes back even further. In Ed Catmull's book, Creativity Inc., we learn the story behind this amazing company. Ed, co-founder of Pixar, started with his ideas of computer animation back in the 1970s . He approached Disney, who passed at the time on the idea. He worked with George Lucas for a period of time and then started Pixar in the 1980s. He teamed up with Steve Jobs and the team worked hard for the next decade. They ended up losing over 50 million dollars of Steve Jobs's investment money, but did they quit? No, they did not. They persevered and ultimately came out with the amazing Toy Story in 1995. That movie changed the world of animation forever. Interestingly, Ed Catmull, who was originally turned down by Disney in the early days, is now president of both Pixar and Disney Animation. See what I mean about never quitting?

Thomas Edison and J.P. Morgan

Regarding his repeated failures to perfect the light bulb, Thomas Edison said, "I have not failed. I've just found 10,000 ways that won't work". We all think of Thomas Edison when it comes to the light bulb and lighting up the world. However, J.P. Morgan played a very important role because he put up the money to support the endeavor—against his father's will. Edison and Morgan never quit and because of that we can flip a switch in our home and have light instantly.

Rick Allen

I have had the opportunity to see Def Leppard several times in the past few years and I am always inspired by the history of their band and in particular their drummer, Rick Allen. In December of 1984 the band was climbing high on the music charts when Rick had a car accident and lost his left arm. He initially had his arm reattached but it got infected and things didn't work so his arm was re-amputated.

What's amazing is that he is still the drummer of the band. Don't drummers need both arms? You would think so. That should have been the end of his musical career. But Rick worked with experts to help him find a way to continue with his life's dream and stay a member of the band. They discovered a way to use foot pedals and a specially designed drum kit to help him play all the beats necessary. By 1986 he was back playing with Def Leppard and he continued his climb to rock-and-roll stardom. Rick said, "What I've experienced through losing my arm, I wouldn't change. The human spirit is so strong." The band has sold over 100 million albums worldwide and they continue to tour to today. Rick did not quit and he proved that anything is possible. If the dream is strong enough, we as humans will always find a way.

James Lawrence

Not giving up is absolutely key in the world of sports as well. All sports are filled with stories of men and women who did not give up on their dreams and therefore ended up achieving their dreams, often against tough odds. I want to highlight someone you may not yet be familiar with. His name is James Lawrence, aka the "Iron Cowboy." I have known James through the triathlon community in Utah and our families are friends from our home country of Canada. In 2012, James set the world record in both half ironman distance and full ironman distance events in one year (30 full-ironman distance events in 11 countries—simply amazing).

However amazing this achievement was, he wanted to take it to an entirely new level. He set his sights on 50 full-distance triathlons (Ironman distance) in 50 consecutive days in all 50 US states. That is 2.4 miles of swimming, 112 miles of biking followed by a 26.2 mile run each day for 50 days, with the additional challenge of having to travel to a new state each day. Wow.

James prepped for several years and on July 25th of 2015 he crossed the finish line having swam a total of 120 miles, biked 5,603 miles and ran 1,310 miles (and traveled thousands more to get to each state!). The experience was, as you can imagine, very difficult at times. I had the opportunity and blessing of joining James for one of his 50 events in Muncie, Indiana.

He told me that the first three days of racing, he was operating on around 7 hours of sleep total. Imagine that. On day 18 in Tennessee, he was so exhausted that he fell asleep on his bike and crashed. Despite crashing he still finished that day and continued the next. There were many times I am sure the idea of quitting crossed his mind. But an athlete who has set out to accomplish specific dreams feed their dreams so much that it truly crowds out any fears and crushes the desire to quit. The moment the thought of quitting enters, these athletes are able to drown out that noise with their strong desire to succeed with their dreams. James is a great example of that.

Another point of interest in James' experience was that during each event, many local athletes joined in the racing just to experience it with James and show him support. James said on several occasions to people that the main rule of running with him was to engage only in positive discussions. Negativity was not allowed. As an elite athlete, James understands this principle instinctively. He knows that to accomplish something great, he needs to control his input. He did not want to chance allowing negative to enter into his world and take root. The date that he crossed the final finish line in Utah, James had accomplished something no other human being had ever done. Being with James during his day 40 in Muncie, Indiana was truly one of the more inspiring experiences in my life.

I could go on and on with more examples of people achieving their dreams, but the point is this that we depend on those who do not quit on their dreams. Drive down any main street in your town and look at each of the businesses along that street. Behind each of them is a story of an entrepreneur or group of entrepreneurs who refuse to quit on their dreams. So why should it be any different for you? There is always a way and the world depends on us to not give up and find that way.

There is no shortage of people who will tell you that dreams don't come true and to not waste your time and energy on going after your dreams. "Live in the box" is what they are really telling you. But we rely on the "out of the box" thinkers. There is no shortage of people who quit on their dreams. Don't be one of these people. If you follow the steps of dream building outlined in this chapter, you will find success and you will find your dreams coming true. Take the time and make the effort and it will happen for you.

Don't Quit

When things go wrong as they sometimes will,
When the road you are trudging seems all uphill,
When the funds are low and the debts are high,
And you want to smile but you have to sigh,
When care is pressing you down a bit,
Rest if you must but don't you quit.

(This isn't part of the poem, but here you can add in your mind, "There's always a way.")

Life is queer with its twists and turns,
As every one of us sometimes learns,
And many a fellow turns about,
When he might have won had he stuck it out.

Don't give up though the pace seems slow–
You may succeed with another blow.

Often the goal is nearer than
It seems to a faint and faltering man,
Often the struggler has given up,
When he might have captured the victor's cup;
And he learned too late when the night came down,
How close he was to the golden crown.

Success is failure turned inside out–
The silver tint in the clouds of doubt,
And you never can tell how close you are,
It might be near when it seems afar;
So stick to the fight when you're hardest hit–
Rest if you must but don't you quit.

(There's always a way.)

– Author unknown

CHAPTER 8

Take Care of Your Body

How we feel inside will show on the outside. Our physical health affects us in all we do, including whether we are positive or negative. It affects us in all the roles we play. We need to be on our "A" game in every area, and our physical health is no exception. So here are a few thoughts on how striving for optimal health can help you along your journey. I have purposely not gone into a lot of detail. There are hundreds of books and websites that can give you far more detailed information. However, what I'm including here will hopefully help you think a bit about how important health really is, which can ultimately help you make some relatively quick decisions that can make profound impact.

My father used an analogy with us growing up to teach us this point. If the fire alarm goes off in the house we can rip the alarm out of wall. That is a "semi-solution" that takes away the annoyance of the sound but doesn't get rid of the fire. It is clear, however, that eventually the fire is going to catch up to us.

And so it is with our health. We have become conditioned to look for answers to our health problems that merely take away the annoyance of specific symptoms that truly do nothing to fix the real problem (the fire) that is creating the symptom.

Most pharmaceutical drugs don't address the source problem—they just mask the noise that is coming from the source. I am not saying there is not a place for drugs, but I am saying once again that the answers are within, if we will but only look.

Sleep Is Critical

Lack of sleep and the challenges that are associated with lack of sleep is like a fire going off that we can quiet with drugs of all sorts (caffeine anyone?), but it doesn't solve the problem, which could be as easy as this—get more sleep. We know instinctively that we need a solid night's sleep each day. We don't need a professional or some study to teach us this. It is biological. It is how we have been designed. We need this time each and every day to repair physically, emotionally, spiritually and mentally. However, we have become so overworked, over-stressed and overwhelmed as a human race that in general we either don't get sufficient amount of sleep or we have a hard time sleeping period.

This lack of sleep is affecting our productivity in all the roles that we play in our lives. Lack of sleep is affecting our moods, our relationships, our performance on the job and other areas, our positive outlook, our enthusiasm about what we are doing, our spirituality, our health and even our weight (yes, proper sleep helps us as we are seeking a healthy weight). If you are consistently not getting enough sleep there is not enough caffeine to get your brain straight in the long run. God has created our bodies in such a way to address the repair that is needed daily. I am not saying there is not a place for caffeine or other products to help us with our energy and cognitive function. I am simply saying that the caffeine or drugs many of us use to prop ourselves up should not be the solution each and every day to compensate for our lack of sleep. That can only last so long before we "break."

How Can We Calm Ourselves and Sleep Better?

It is becoming increasingly more difficult to shut off the constant chatter that exists in our minds. The practices of Taking 5 before bed, particularly gratitude, love, being present/meditation and reading something positive and that will feed your dreams, will help calm your mind, body and spirit and prepare you for a proper night's sleep.

I also like to seek natural methods of calming myself prior to sleep. It is very helpful to take a warm bath before retiring. Warm water, some calming bath salts, candles and/or essential oils such as lavender or chamomile accompanied by a book is a good way to finish a day and prepare your body for a night of repair. Another thing I like to do is to make a cup of chamomile herbal tea. I prefer the loose-leaf tea that I can brew myself. Very tasty and very calming and I find loose leaf to be more effective. Melatonin supplements can also be helpful. Melatonin is naturally produced in our bodies, helping us regulate sleep patterns. However, the older we become the less we produce. As children we produce more melatonin, which is one of the reasons why a child can fall asleep so easily. Melatonin is also a very good antioxidant. Seek to get a minimum of 7-8 hours each and every night and watch your life transform to a more positive world.

Your Health Is a Reflection of What You Eat

Our internal guidance system tells us that what we put into our mouths from the time it enters, goes through our digestive system, gets absorbed (or doesn't get absorbed) and then what gets sent out the other end has an effect on our health and wellness. My brother Gordon likes to point out that if you don't believe this, go eat an entire bag of prunes. The results will certainly help you believe this statement.

So what are you to do when it comes to your dietary choices? There are so many diets and experts saying "eat this" and "do this" for weight loss, or for more energy, or for better body sculpting. How is one to know what to do? The answer is so easy and yet so remarkably complex. I say "complex" because there are so many opinions from experts telling us what and how to eat. My purpose with this segment is to simply awaken awareness and help you be conscious of this on your journey. Details will come to you as you search for better health and wellness, which will indeed help you live a more positive and healthy lifestyle. Here it is:

1. Eat a balanced variety of clean-sourced proteins, carbohydrates and fats

2. Eat as many whole foods as possible, which means:

 - Limit or eliminate processed foods

 - Limit or eliminate processed sugar

3. If something doesn't agree with you, then don't eat it. Don't take a drug so you can eat what doesn't agree with you. Don't suppress it—avoid it.

There you have it. Of course there are books written about each subject and as many details as you could possibly want exist on these subjects if you want to dive deeper. But I like to simplify in life. This is about what it comes down to. Our bodies are designed to function on a healthy balance of protein, carbs and fats. Yes, I did say fats. Yes, I did say carbohydrates. Yes I did say protein. My rule of thumb is that if someone preaches a strong emphasis on any one area and excludes or highly limits the other(s), they are preaching a fad and the long-term results won't be good.

Balance and clean sources are key. What do I mean by clean source? Deep-fried chicken versus grilled chicken. Doughnuts versus a pear. A homemade salad dressing with olive oil and vinegar as opposed to a processed store brand. A general rule of thumb that I try to follow is to have more than 3/4 of my plate be vegetables—preferably green veggies. Eat whole sources of fruits and vegetables. This supplies you with the important fiber needed to properly process your nutrition. Common sense. Eat as Mother Nature intended you to eat—foods in their natural, unprocessed state.

Fats Are Important

I do want to say something about fat. The word "fat" has been demonized since the middle of the 20th century. We were lead to believe that fat was the source of most of our problems. Hence the food companies started pulling fat out of our foods. Interestingly the foods did not taste so good, so what did they do? They added more sugar. Sugar went on the rise and fat went on the decline. Which only lead to the recent discovery that fats are necessary for optimal health and wellness in all areas, including energy, brain health and even weight management. Learn which fats are good for you. Avocados, olive oil, coconut oil, fats from nuts and seeds, fish fats and so forth are the generally necessary fats. Again, use common sense when it comes to fat—eat whole foods from clean sources.

Sugar Hurts Us

Sugar is naturally found in fruits and vegetables. However, the sugar I want to discuss is the "processed" sugar that is added to our food in huge amounts. Around the year 1900, the average American ate around 5-10 pounds of sugar per year. Today it is estimated to be a startling .25 to .5 lbs per day. That is 90-180 pounds per year for the average American. It's clear—we are "over sugared" in our society. And it is affecting our health and wellness, including our positive outlook on life. Why do I say that? Because if we are not feeling well it simply brings us down.

When we eat sugar, chemicals called opioids and beta-endorphins are released and cause us to feel good. This is the "sugar rush" you often hear about. Sugar affects our brains in the same way as nicotine and cocaine. It doesn't last long, which is why we become addicted to the constant hit of more sugar. Which is why, of course, so many of us are addicted and we don't even know it. The more you eat high sugar foods, the more you want to eat more sugary foods. It is highly addictive.

Sugar drains our energy, dulls our senses, contributes to the cardiovascular problems we see today, promotes the obesity epidemic as well as diabetes, and a whole host of other health challenges (including emotional dysfunction). How can sugar have become such a problem? The answer is in what our food companies are marketing to us starting at such an early age of our children.

Increase Water to Decrease Sugar

One way to drop your sugar intake starting today is to choose water. This is a fairly simple principle to understand but tougher to implement. So many choices are before us each and every day. Marketing campaigns are bombarding us to have us choose their soft drink or "fruit drink" or energy drink. What to do? But you almost always have a choice on how to hydrate. Your body is approximately 70% water. Choose water. Along these lines, I always start my day with a full glass of water and, if possible, add lemon to it. Lemon helps balance your PH. And it tastes great.

Sugar as an example is an interesting study. What used to be considered a treat in decades past is now found in the vast majority of foods that most Americans eat every meal in every day. Just do a little research on the negative effects of sugar on human health. You want to make a quick difference to help you live a more positive life? Then educate yourself and make a decision to stop or seriously limit your intake of added sugar in your diet.

One place to start is a movie called "That Sugar Film." It's a great educational tool that I highly recommend.

Chew Your Food

We have become so busy in our world that we forget a very fundamental need, which is to properly chew our food before swallowing. Again, basic information that we should not need a study or some expert to explain to us. We hear the saying, "We are what we eat." How about we also are what we eat and are able to digest? Your body needs proteins, carbs and fats. It knows then to discard what it doesn't need. However if we are eating so quickly and chewing just a few times before swallowing then we are putting enormous pressure on our digestive system to try and get what it needs to nourish the body with the nutrients and fuel that come from the protein, carbs and fats. This is something you can do starting today to get on a road to improving your health, and it will give you more clarity of mind and energy.

So again, chew your food. Some say a good rule of thumb is to chew thirty times before swallowing. But I say chew until you are ready to swallow. Listen to your body. You will know. I will say that if you are eating a steak and you chew 2-10 times it is mostly likely not even close. Take smaller bites and chew. Give your digestive system as much help as you can to do its job by chewing properly. You will also find yourself enjoying your meal more by savoring each bite. What a blessing food truly is.

Along these same lines, be careful not to overeat. This one is a little tougher because eating is so pleasurable. I know because I love to eat. That is normal. Your body will tell you when you have had enough but you need to break things up for your body to truly signal you. While you are eating your body is saying, "Bring it on, this is great. Keep it coming," and it potentially will until it is too late. But at that point you will likely be so full you are falling asleep as your digestive system is overloaded, trying to digest it all. Here is a solution. Try to stop eating about half way through your meal and wait ten minutes. Talk to people if you are with them. If you are by yourself, then maybe read or just relax by getting into the present. If you are feeling like you need more food after ten minutes, eat a little more (while of course chewing it well), but then stop again and let your body tell you. We need to listen to our bodies more and not take a pill that will allow us to eat more than we should or eat stuff that does not agree with our body.

Mother Nature Knows

Volumes of books in cultures from all over the world have been dedicated to what Mother Nature has put on this earth to help us with our health and wellness, including healing ourselves. These botanicals are all around us and in most cases go unnoticed. For example, to most people dandelions are a nuisance. We spray them and try to get rid of them. Not my mother. She would pick the dandelion leaves and make salads for us. They are a bit bitter but so good for our health. The dandelion has been used and is still used for myriad of health, wellness and healing, ranging from internal detoxification to external antibacterial benefits. It is such a powerful botanical that is literally right below our eyes, yet all too often unnoticed. My mother had a peppermint bush outside our house, another botanical that is prolific in its growing and often times seen as a weed. Yet, the healing benefits of peppermint are great. For example, peppermint can aid in digestion, something that so many people could use. Isn't it interesting that in life it is often times the small, simple and seemingly ordinary things that turn out to be so very powerful and extraordinary? Consider the words of the great Hippocrates who said thousands of years ago, "Let food be your medicine and medicine be your food." This opens our minds to the massive possibility that what we need just very well may be right before us.

I have suffered several broken bones. When I broke my bones I did not try to put some herbs on it to heal. Instead, I went to experts in the medical community to help mend my broken bones, and how grateful I am to modern science for these amazing possibilities. We are blessed. However, for most healing that I seek in my life I look towards my "foods," or shall I say botanicals, to help me along my healing path. These amazing botanicals have been put on this earth for a purpose and how blessed we are that so many have been discovered over the centuries by cultures all over the world and studied so we don't need to look very far to find solutions. I encourage you to have a herb/botanical bible of sorts at your fingertips. You will be amazed at what is there ready and waiting for your use and benefit. Mother Nature really does know what we need and has put it before us for our use. We just need to seek it out and apply it in or lives.

Be Active. Stay Active.

Again, this is something we know. There are so many opinions on this subject. But it can be so overwhelming, so what to do? Again, this is not meant to cover lots of details but rather to provide some of my basic thoughts on this subject to help you potentially make a quick decision that could alter your positive outlook in very quick order:

1. Newton's law of motion states: "Every object in a state of uniform motion tends to remain in that state of motion unless an external force is applied to it."

In other words, get "in motion" and you'll more easily stay in motion.

2. Use it or lose it. In all my years of endurance sports and other activities, I've endured different injuries. Consequently, I can testify that muscle atrophy is very real. If you don't use your muscles, you really will lose them. After just a few short months of being in a cast the atrophy was very noticeable. Anyone who has had a cast can appreciate this.

3. Oxygen is life giving. The principle here is quite basic. Get moving by doing something. It doesn't matter what it is. This is relative to everyone. Find out what you like to do and do it! Is that running, hiking or walking? For some, yes. So run, walk or bike and enjoy it. Is it weight lifting? For some, yes. So do it and enjoy it. Is it dancing? Then dance your heart out. Is it biking? Go for it. Rock climbing? Go for it. Swimming? Yoga? Pilates? Hot yoga? Whatever it may be, do it, do it consistently and enjoy it. If you are worried for your health, then speak to your doctor first but move toward a plan. Enjoy muscle activity and the cardiovascular benefits as well as the overall more positive outlook on life. Endorphins will kick in, which are mother nature's feel-good medicine. And here's the thing—you are already equipped for that to happen. You just may need to remind yourself how to activate it. You have been created with these feel-good medicines naturally found within. You are a miracle.

CONCLUSION

In the first chapter of this book, I introduced the idea of "Positive In, Positive Out." What this means is that if we program our minds and hearts with positivity (Positive In), then positive will come out (Positive Out). As you enter this new world of putting positive in so that positive will flow out in all the roles you have in life, you will be reminded how important you are. Each of us is important in so many ways, and in order to be happy and successful we have to believe it! Let me give you an example using one of my favorite movies.

There are many classics that I enjoy watching during the Christmas season. One in particular is It's a Wonderful Life. I enjoy this film for many reasons. Number one, my wife and I watched it together while we were deciding on marriage. I like to believe it helped me with the process, so I am grateful. Second, our three boys were in a production of this play several years ago and we were blessed to watch it for several months during practices as well as performances. No matter how many times I watched it, I never got tired of the message. Third, I believe we are drawn to the message of this film because we all feel a bit like George Bailey. Life can beat us down and the day-to-day experience of life can cause us to truly question whether there is any purpose to it all.

The movie strikes a chord with people because we can relate to the main character and what he experiences. Allow me to recap the story briefly for you. George Bailey, played by Jimmy Stewart, grew up in a small town named Bedford Falls. He had many dreams and aspirations in life to build a fortune and travel the world. The story highlights a few key moments in his early life that, although seemingly insignificant at the time, will have a profound impact later. George watches his friends make it big in the world while he remains faithful to helping his father's business in Bedford Falls. He watches his brother go to war and become a hero, while once again he is left back in Bedford Falls to support the war effort from home. When he finally gets the chance to move on in his life, his father passes away and George has to remain home and continue to run the family business. All these life events leave him feeling frustrated. He feels like he is making no impact on the world. He does marry and raise a family, but all the while he is feeling less and less fulfilled.

There comes a point in the story when a series of unfortunate events leads George to misplace some very important funds needed for his business. The loss of these funds will result in him having some serious problems with the law. He feels like life is no longer worth it and attempts to take his life. At this point God sends him an angel by the name of Clarence. In the presence of Clarence, George utters the words, "I wish I were never born." Clarence decides to grant him his wish—a gift to see what the world would be like if George Bailey had never been born.

This is a very interesting point in the story. Have you ever considered what life would be like if you had never been born? It is easy to get caught up in thinking that we make no difference in this world. I believe this is one of the main reasons why It's a Wonderful Life is such a beautiful story, because the viewer starts to go there in their mind with their own lives. The director, Frank Capra, takes us on a journey of what life would be like had George never been born. For example, during the war his younger brother was a war hero saving the lives on many soldiers. However, if George had never been born, during a childhood accident he would not have saved his brother's life, therefore his brother would never have saved the lives of those soldiers.

Another profound example is the effect on a man George worked for at the local pharmacy. Without George around, his boss made a grave error that cost the life of one of his patients. But with George in his life, he made a better decision that saved this person's life. George helped keep his boss from going to prison and becoming an alcoholic. The town was also completely different because George Bailey kept his father's vision with the savings and loan institution that offered affordable housing to hard working folks who couldn't quite afford a home otherwise. His children, who meant the world to George, were never born because he and his wife never married. His wife grew old, having never married. At one point, while going through the horror of what he is observing, Clarence the angel says, "Strange, isn't it? Each man's life touches so many other lives. When he isn't around, he leaves an awful hole, doesn't he? You see, George, you really did have a wonderful life. Don't you see what a mistake it would be to throw it away?" George does see, and at this point he prays to have his life back, challenges and all.

My friend, I want you to know that you too really do have a wonderful life. You are blessed beyond measure. You have talents and abilities that are needed to make a difference in this world. We all need to be woken up to this understanding. We don't need to have our life wiped away in the form of a dream for us to truly recognize our worth. Sadly, many people go throughout life as if in a trance, never waking to the reality that they are truly powerful beyond comprehension. We often seek happiness through external sources, thinking that the next purchase, or the next program, or the next degree, or the next relationship, or the next job, or the next whatever, will be the solution. But no, it is something much more internal than that. Finding real happiness happens the moment we recognize the power inside us, the power we have had all along, just waiting to be discovered.

Sages from the beginning of time have taught this truth. Buddha said, "Look within. Be still. Free from fear and attachment, know the sweet joy of living in the way." Lao Tzu said, "The journey of a thousand miles starts under one's feet." Marcus Aurelius said, "Very little is needed to make a happy life; it is all within yourself, in your way of thinking." Mahatma Gandhi said, "Be the change you want to see in this world." In the Gospel of Thomas it says, "If you bring forth what is within you, what you bring forth will save you. If you do not bring forth what is within you, what you do not bring forth will destroy you." The Sikh Holy Prayer from the Golden Temple, Amritsar, India, says, "My Lord is everywhere and omnipresent. We search all over but within. My Lord is right there in me. Let us open our inner eyes to see and accept that God is in us and I am only an extension of his entity." And Jesus said, "Neither shall they say, Lo here! Or lo there! For behold, the kingdom of God is within you."

Seek Serenity for Positivity

Life is an amazing journey with all its ups and downs. Challenges will come and go. No one is immune to challenges, including me. But when I was confronted with a major obstacle, I eventually chose gratitude. I chose love. I chose to live in the moment. I chose to fill my mind with positive and shut out the negative. I chose to dream. And in doing so, I chose to live.

What I have learned in my journey, not even knowing it, was that I was seeking through my exercise, endurance sports and mountain climbing and camping to shut out the world and quiet my mind. Now I do these activities knowing this and my ability to quiet my mind and turn within is so much more amplified. I find solitude, quiet and beauty in my exercise. Being on a mountain, whether it be hiking or camping or mountaineering, gives me the opportunity and blessing to shut off my phone, shut out the external chatter and turn within. Where I used to stress about not being able to connect to my phone and office, I realized that with that stress I was missing out on the very moment I was experiencing. Now I welcome the solitude and open my soul to inspiration.

As Rumi once said, "Silence is God's language. Everything else is poor translation." I now welcome any moment to silence my mind. The key is to recognize it and tap in. I now welcome the solitude of an airplane ride or a hotel stay. How blessed I am to have these moments to read, write, study, pray and meditate on life and the blessings and challenges that life brings. No longer do I allow my mind to dwell on thoughts like, "What if I just did that?" or "What if he or she just did that or said that?" No longer do I allow my mind to wander to the point where I utter the words, "That isn't fair" or "If only I would have" or "I should have." Life just is. If I find myself turning negative or dwelling on the past or whatever causes me these emotions that I no longer want in my life, then I recognize and acknowledge it, and use the techniques found in this book to break the pattern and move forward in a positive direction. It works. I want to live my life in such a way that no matter what life throws my way, I calmly approach it with a desire to learn and grow.

As you learn to accept life with all its great times and not-so-great times and embrace the lessons that life has to teach you, then you will learn the true art of taking a deep breath and saying silently or out loud, "Life is truly a blessing."

We have a strong inner guidance system to help us. First, we must realize that we are divine creations meant for greatness. Second, we have to recognize what it takes to pull us out of whatever we are experiencing. Third, we must go in the direction of what dominates our minds so that we better choose what we put into our minds and into our hearts. With this we are prepared to accomplish our dreams, whatever they may be.

Practicing "Positive In" with the "Take 5" steps as a guide each and every day will help awaken you to a new world of possibility. Don't hesitate. Start today and watch your days, weeks, months and years transform. Thank you for reading this book and I invite you to make each day what you want it to be. You, my friend, are in control.

Made in the USA
San Bernardino, CA
31 May 2016